Location, Location, Location

That's Not Right, Do It Again

It's Not About Persuasion

Things I Did for Love

Obedience to the Law
Is Freedom

Follow Your Damn Bliss

Pretty Pictures

Advanced Nitrate
Propellents

Girls, Bunnies & America

Tombstone

Done Is Better Than Prefect

Victore

or,

Who Died and Made You Boss?

Introduction by
Michael Bierut

Design by
Office of Paul Sahre

Abrams, New York

Marcel Duchamp
Rrose Sélavy
Jose Guadalupe Posada
Lucian Bernhard
Maimonides
Bob Wills
Jack Teagarden
Caravaggio
Carl Rogers
Fred McFeely Rogers
Johnny Cash
Abebe Bikila
Pepe, Punch, and Primo
Primo Carnera
Dr. Seuss
Dr. Spock, not the Vulcan
James Montgomery "Jimmy" Doohan, the Scotty
Bessie Smith
Steve McQueen
Francisco "Paco" Bultó, for the Bultaco
Bert Lahr
Groucho, Harpo, and Chico Marx, but not Zeppo
Margaret Dumont, for her tolerance of the Marx Brothers
Carmella Montalto
Rose Hamill
Lee Cherry Smith
Chet Baker, for the best make-out music ever
Burt Munro
Levi Strauss
Sam Lucchese Sr.
Eliphalet Remington II
Jackie Stewart
Guillaume Apollinaire the poet
Guillaume Apollinaire the pornographer
Guillaume Apollinaire the art thief
Buddy Holly
Andre Rene Roussimoff, the wrestler, not the sticker
Charles Bukowski
Rodney Dangerfield
Alexander Calder
Steve Prefontaine
Hannah Höch
Jack Johnson, the heavyweight
John Heartfield
Socrates
Christopher Marlowe

Ovid
Kurt Vonnegut
Ed "Big Daddy" Roth
Piero Fornasetti
Eddie Aikau, 'cause he would go
Emil Zátopek
Tristan Tzara
Stephen F. Austin, not the $6 million one
Jacques-Louis David
Colonel Tom Parker, for Elvis
Evel Knievel
Ferdinando Nicola Sacco
Bartolomeo Vanzetti
Paul Rand
Jim McKay
Edith Piaf
Pablo Neruda
E. Anheuser & A. Busch
Farrah Fawcett
Sir William Nicholson and James Pryde
John Bartlett
Freddie Mercury
Mr. Interlocutor and Mr. Bones
Henri de Toulouse-Lautrec
Woody Guthrie, because his machine kills fascists
George Bernard Shaw
George Herriman, and his krazy fucking kat
George Carlin, for his seven words, not his ads
Robert Shaw
Jeff Buckley
Francisco Goya
Saul Steinberg
Victor Borge
Winston Churchill
Salvador Dali, for his moustache, not his painting
Franz Kline, for his painting, not his moustache
Rockwell Kent
E. E. Cummings
Honoré de Balzac, for the greatest last name ever
Auguste Rodin, for his Balzac
William James
Joseph Campbell
George Orwell
Dalton Trumbo
Whoever invented the cigar
Jack London

Vincent van Gogh
Rainer Maria Rilke
Honoré Daumier
David Foster Wallace
Roman Cieslewicz
Eugéne Delacroix
Vladimir Vladimirovich Nabokov
Katsushika Hokusai
Anne Sexton
Louis Armstrong, for the Hot Fives and Sevens
Edward Lear
Puccini, for making romance of poverty, and beautifully
Yukio Mishima
Mark Rothko
Maxfield Parrish
Henry Moore
Rudyard Kipling, for "If"
Buddha
Muhammad
Jesus
Lao Tzu, but not Sun Tzu
Confucius, but not the fortune cookie one
Stanley Kubrick
Andy Warhol
Joan Miró
Philip Guston
Aldous Huxley, for our future
George W. Bush
Tecumseh, for his writing, not the two stroke engine
James Thurber, for his world
Ned Ludd
Flannery O'Conner
Patrick Swayze, but only for Road House
A. J. Liebling
Lefty Frizzell
Paavo Nurmi
Dale Earnhardt
Frankie, of course
John Barrymore and the whole damn clan
Marcel Broodthaers
Robert Frost
The Sumerians, for inventing beer
The Benedictine monk, Dom Pérignon
Indian Larry
"Spider" Sabich
Hank Williams

Alfred Nobel, for his dynamite, not the Peace Prize
Charlie Chaplin
William Wallace
James J. Braddock
Orson Welles
William Earnest Henley, for "Invictus"
Arthur Lydiard, for the lactic acid
D. W. Griffith
John Ford
"Sam" Peckinpah
Stirling Moss
Walt Disney, just kidding
Alexis-Charles-Henri Clérel de Tocqueville
Walter Cronkite
Richard Pryor, because white folks are funny
Waylon Jennings
Walt Whitman, for his love of Mannahatta
Gil Elvgren
Louis Prima, life goes on without him
Wallace Gordon "Wally" Parks
Topo Gigo
Serge Gainsbourg
Akira Kurosawa
Toshiro Mifune
John Belushi
Charles Nelson, USMC
Robert Mitchum
Simon John Ritchie
John Graham Mellor
Candy Jernigan
Charles Laughton, with or without the hump
Marty Feldman, with the hump
Robert Rauschenberg
Rita Hayworth, for Gilda
John Cage, for about four minutes
Bob Keeshan, thanks for everything.

Library of Congress Cataloging-in-Publication Data

Victore, James, 1962–

Victore or, Who died and made you boss?/ by James Victore ; introduction by Michael Bierut.

p. cm.

Includes bibliographical references and index.

ISBN 978-0-8109-9591-8 (hardcover : alk. paper)

1. Victore, James, 1962– —Themes, motives. I. Title. II. Title: Who died and made you boss?

NC999.4.V53A4 2010
741.6092—dc22   2009049348

Printed and bound in Hong Kong, China
10 9 8 7 6 5 4 3 2 1

Abrams books are available at special discounts when purchased in quantity for premiums and promotions as well as fundraising or educational use. Special editions can also be created to specification. For details, contact specialmarkets@abramsbooks.com, or the address below.

ABRAMS

115 West 18th Street
New York, NY 10011
www.abramsbooks.com

Sincerely,

To Joseph Victore, who taught me
how to be a man and a father

To Luca Victore, always do what is
in your heart, and keep smiling

Preface

This book is not about graphic design. It is not filled with pretty pictures made in the service of a host of concerns that are not my own. I have always tried to make work that has an opinion. My opinion. Since the beginning of my career I have done a very good job of shooting myself in the foot professionally. I'm sure this book will be no different.

I didn't set out here to create a catalogue of every single job I have ever done, but rather to provide something of a "greatest hits" compilation. Everyone makes crap, and I'm no exception; out of respect, however, I will shelter you from my more egregious indiscretions. I have selected forty-eight projects and presented them here, in roughly chronological order, along with the stories and ideas behind their making—as unrealistic or blasphemous as they may seem. For the most part, I have chosen not to describe why I've employed particular imagery, typography, and so on, focusing instead on my attempts to make work that excites me and, hopefully, in turn, you.

I strive for one thing in my work: to make it personal. I believe that, as a graphic designer, if you do a good job of telling your own story, putting your experience, your knowledge, and your life into your work, it will resonate with your audience. Simply put, in the particular lies the universal. If I am too careful not to offend, too worried about what the client will think, or, even worse, if I become a stooge for marketing concerns, and forget to bring my sense of play or poetry to the work, how can I expect the public to get excited? It is through applying this philosophy to my work that I've managed, over the years, to forge a reputation as someone who creates moving images and powerful messages for himself, for an audience, and for a client.

This book is not about art. I am a graphic designer, a commercial artist. I work in a business, but the saddest three words in the English language are, "It's just business." Because of

For the past twenty-five years I have worked in almost every format graphic design encompasses, but my preferred tool—and what this book celebrates most—is the poster. For me, the poster has always been the simplest and bluntest format in which to work (not to mention that it's often the biggest)—like a large spiked club. Unlike other design formats, the poster doesn't need the official stamp of a client; it can live on its own. As proof of a certain democracy, it stands on the street with nothing but an idea behind it. The great French designer A. M. Cassandre said, "A good poster enters through the eye and explodes in the brain." In the history of images that move people, the poster has been—and continues to be—the tool of choice to attract attention, excite people, and even to change the world.

Victore is my family name, my father's name, but I never intended it to be the title of my first book. The title I intended, which I came up with when I was ten years old and which is now this book's subtitle, was *Who Died and Made You Boss?* This question was often posed during my childhood when I had stepped beyond my bounds. Today that question is as relevant as ever: "Who indeed?" The answer is no one. Not in life or in work. No one gives you permission. Freedom is something that you take.

At a lecture I gave, a designer plaintively explained to me that while he wanted to do creative work, he had rent to pay. "Fuck rent!" was my loud response. To give a damn is a personal calling, not a job description. Just make the work and nail it up on a wall.

—James Victore

business, and primarily the fear of losing it, clients—and in turn, designers—cannot afford to have an opinion. What a lousy position to be in! How can anybody make anything of value without an opinion? You can't do good work for a client who is afraid of telling the truth, and following the money almost always leads to poor work. With this book, I offer a body of work largely unsullied by financial reward.

I have always called myself an "independent designer." To me, this means making choices—choices between work and life, what jobs I do and with whom I do them, and when to fire a client. I have purposefully designed my life so I have the freedom to spend the maximum amount of time with my wife and son. I do not want to have to choose between work and family.

I'd have to be a complete charlatan to present this book as if to say, "Look at me and my great work." These projects are the result of working with clients who are interested in fighting the good fight. I use the word *clients* a lot in these pages, but I really mean comrades.

Over the years I have been spoiled; I've worked with smart, sexy, brave people, organizations, and companies who want to make powerful statements. When a project comes into the studio, I claim the right of coauthor. If there is no collaboration, there is no good work. If the client is not interested in loosening the reins and trusting me, then they are not the right client.

Introduction

There are some things you remember clearly almost twenty years later. It was the early nineties. I was dropping something off at the receptionist's desk in our office. And there, popping out amidst the clutter on her desk, was a business card for a theater group. I picked it up. "This is nice!" I said to our receptionist, Elizabeth. She was an aspiring actress making ends meet by answering our phones.

Elizabeth was startled. "Really?"

"Yeah," I said. "I wonder who designed it."

The next day she had the answer. "Here, I wrote it down, but I don't know how to pronounce it." And there on the card she offered was written a name completely unfamiliar to me.

"Wow, I've never heard of him," I said. I looked again at the card. "He's really good."

"He is?" asked Elizabeth, genuinely puzzled. "How can you tell?"

The name, of course, was James Victore. And the question remains: how can you tell?

It sometimes seems there are two kinds of graphic designers in the world. One kind sees each project as an opportunity for self-expression, producing a body of work that bears an unmistakable mark, that is more alike than different, that is more about the maker than the message. At its best, the output of this kind of designer is personal and passionate; at worst, it's repetitive and self-indulgent, the mark of the attention-seeking diva.

The other kind of designer attends first to the client, to the message, and to the audience. This graphic designer's role is to be neutral and invisible, an efficient conduit between broadcaster and receiver. The best of this kind of work is devastatingly effective; the worst is anonymous and forgettable, the product of the kind of hack who gives design a bad name.

James Victore is good because, amazingly, he combines the very best of both ways. His work is unmistakably his. Every one of his pieces bears his handwriting. More often than not, this is literally true: few designers have done more to render typography foundries irrelevant than Victore. The human hand, his hand, is always in evidence. Yet this signature approach takes so many different tones. His handlettering can evoke Spencerian script or the scrawl of a stickup man, a puff of cigar smoke or a mushroom cloud. All of it, though, has one thing in common. It conveys the sense that the words don't want to wait around to be put into type, justified, and kerned. Instead, the ideas are rushing to get out.

And there lies the paradox that makes Victore so hard to classify. His work, so personal, conveys ideas with the directness of a speeding freight train. If his intention is to shock, as sometimes it is, it is because the subject matter—racism, the death penalty, unsafe sex—is shocking. The results can be shockingly funny as well: just ask the subscribers to a leading design magazine who were given a quick and viciously literal lesson on the difference between Shinola and its customary opposite. And don't expect an apology if you're offended. You won't get one. Nor will you ever, ever miss the point.

If one were envious, one might shrug off Victore for taking the easy way out. After all, he works with art schools, cultural groups, worthy causes, the kind of clients one might think would offer ideal opportunities for memorable design solutions. However, people who talk dismissively about shooting fish in a barrel have probably never taken aim at one of those slippery devils: it's harder, and messier, than you think. Victore has the powder burns to show for it. And in the midst of those celebrated big bold ideas, all delivered with fierce and accurate punches, one is always surprised to find an example of beautifully structured information design. For example, turn over what is perhaps Victore's most celebrated poster, featuring a game of hangman that's completed to devastating effect in the viewer's head. There on the back is a sober typographic treatment of the poster's subject, Racism and the Death Penalty, laid out with the straightforward clarity of a brochure for Swiss pharmaceuticals. The two sides of one talented designer were never so perfectly illustrated.

Beatrice Warde once described the two kinds of designers with an extended metaphor in her celebrated 1955 essay "The Crystal Goblet, or Printing Should Be Invisible." Some designers, she wrote, create solutions that are like elaborate wine goblets, "solid gold, wrought in the most exquisite patterns." These are the expressive designers who let their personalities get in the way. Others prefer to pour wine into a "crystal-clear glass, thin as a bubble, and as transparent." These are the neutral designers, desperate to stay in the background.

So let's make this simple. Here's how you can tell this designer is good. James Victore does away with the goblets altogether. He simply wrenches the cork off the bottle and pours the stuff right down your throat.

Are you thirsty? I know I am. Cheers.

—Michael Bierut

Early Book Covers

While I was growing up, my mother worked in the reference department of the local university library. I'd go there after school to await the ride home, and, knowing I loved to draw, my mother would entertain me with stacks of art- and design-history books. I learned to love books and unconsciously began my education during those hours. At eleven years old, I was looking at posters that were a part of American and world history. Posters that inspired some youths to fight for their country and others to protest war. In a poster book I first saw Tommie Smith raise his gloved fist in support of Black Power from the podium of the 1968 Olympics. I saw the moving and painterly images from all fronts of World War II. It was in those books that I first saw the works of John Heartfield, Tadanori Yokoo, Peter Max, Andy Warhol, as well as Grapus, and images from Mai '68. My eyes grew wide. There were advertising posters that were seductive and beautiful, which advertised tea and soap. I saw contemporary images from Poland and Japan that bore no resemblance to anything I had ever seen before. And I wanted to be involved. At nineteen, I packed a bag of clothes and took a bus to New York City.

At twenty-one, I had already dropped out of art school—my second go at college. I went seeking career advice from one of my former type instructors, a dapper book jacket designer named Paul Bacon. Paul has the kind of talent that is not applauded in our business anymore; he is a designer-illustrator. Paul can paint, draw typography, take beautiful photos, design striking book covers, and illustrate—a master of his trade. Most memorable among his works are book covers for the likes of Ernest Hemingway, William Golding, Norman Mailer, Kurt Vonnegut, and E. L. Doctorow, as well as his covers for *Portnoy's Complaint, Catch-22, One Flew Over the Cuckoo's Nest, and Zen and the Art of Motorcycle Maintenance.*

Since I was practically reared in a university library and already had a great love for books, publishing seemed an apt place to start my career. Fortunately—despite having given me a D in class—Paul agreed to take me on as an apprentice in his small Carnegie Hall studio. From Paul I learned about wine. I learned about cars and auto racing and how to tell a joke so dirty it would singe your eyebrows off. I learned to throw my shoe at talk radio programs. Mostly, I learned about jazz. I learned why Fats Waller is relevant. I learned how good Jelly Roll Morton really is. And also how to listen to Philip Glass, James Brown, even rap. In other words, he taught me everything I needed to know to be a designer. He taught me passion. To look outside of design for inspiration. To seek out the "mad ones." To go out and get the education I needed—to get it from Shakespeare, from music, and from film, yes, but not to overlook motorcycle repair, either.

Thus, for the first years of my career I designed nothing but book covers. Being a freelance designer at that time was a bit like being an itinerant farmhand; I roamed the New York City publishing fields looking for work.

Early on, I took a safe route, making book covers that looked, well, like book covers. It was rare that I worked on novels; most of what I was given involved the less romantic subject matter of alcoholism, the occult, or how to sell a used car. My work got accepted and I got paid. But greatness courts failure. Suddenly emboldened, I began taking chances: making titles too small, the type difficult to read, or using the "wrong" imagery to tell the "right" story. Being young and cocky, I usually signed the front or back of the cover. Collaging, scribbling, searching for a style, and never trying to disguise the handwork or that these marks were made by a human being.

Little by little I was carving out a niche for myself—even if that sometimes meant scaring clients away.

When I pushed too hard and the job was pulled, I'd have to practically live on the kill fees. It was during this period that I failed to make my Faustian deal with the devil. I had made a choice and was unable to yield up creativity for the reward of riches; the two things seemed antithetical. In other words, if I had been a better accountant, I would have understood that I was supposed to be out of business. But I wasn't making business; I was making design. I was experimenting, learning how to fail, and learning how to be comfortable with that.

In the midst of my experimentation, however, I still had to keep myself afloat. In my stepped-up efforts to find work I lugged my portfolio all over, even looking outside the publishing hub of New York City. One of these sorties was via motorcycle to a particularly dingy office in Secaucus, New Jersey, where I met Steve Brower, the art director of Carol Publishing. Steve was not only one of my first clients, but my first comrade. My first ally. I had met someone who not only wanted good work, but would fight for it. An example of Steve's diplomacy came when I delivered to him the design for *Johnny Got His Gun* (Figure 1.15), Dalton Trumbo's searing antiwar novel. After Steve stared at my comp for a moment or two, he said,

"Wait here,"

walked down the hall into his editor's chamber, and closed the door. The ruckus that ensued raised a few curious heads up out of their cubicles, but when Steve came out, red-faced and smiling, he said, "We'll do it."

What I see now in these early covers is the struggle. To make it feel fresh, to make the reader feel the energy, to make it pregnant with emotion. Even today, if my work causes me to laugh or wince, I want the reader to feel that, too. It's a constant fight to get the vision in my head onto the paper, to ensure that a finished piece carries the same energy as the preliminary sketch, and, ultimately, to make a page that may have taken hours to create feel like it was created in an instant.

1.1

The Amateur Astronomer's Handbook
THIRD EDITION
A Guide to Exploring the Heavens
James Muirden
A classic work and a model — *Astronomy*

1.2

Children of Alcoholism
A Survivor's Manual

"Clearly written and moving...
this book will provide comfort,
information and hope."
— *Washington Post*

PL 70010 $6.95

Judith S. Seixes & Geraldine Youcha

MICHAEL KILIAN

A POLITICAL THRILLER

BY ORDER OF THE PRESIDENT

1.3

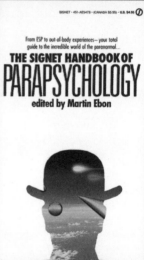

SIGNET · 451 · AE5478 · (CANADA $5.95) · U.S. $4.95

From ESP to out-of-body experiences— your total
guide to the incredible world of the paranormal...

THE SIGNET HANDBOOK OF
PARAPSYCHOLOGY
edited by Martin Ebon

1.4

LARGO DESOLATO

A PLAY BY
Vaclav Havel
ENGLISH VERSION BY
TOM STOPPARD

1.5

Master Plan

Ian Stuart

1.6

**The Case for
Reincarnation**
Joe Fisher
Preface by
The Dalai Lama

1.7

Two plays by
STEVEN **B**ERKOFF

**Kvetch
Acapulco
&**

1.8

ARDENT SPIRITS The Rise
and Fall of
Prohibition
John Kobler

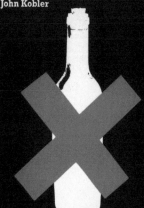

1.9

**JAZZ
SPOKEN
HERE**

Conversations with 22 Musicians
Wayne Enstice & Paul Rubin

1.10

The Creative Mind
An Introduction to
Metaphysics
by Henri Bergson
Winner of the Nobel prize in literature

1+1=3

1.11

ENCYCLOPEDIA OF SIGNS,
OMENS, AND SUPERSTITIONS

Zolar

A spellbinding collection of Occult Lore from the
World-Renowned Astrologer and Spiritualist

1.12

The Talisman
Magick Workbook
by Kala & Ketz Pajeon
*This book will show you how to change your
life, manipulate your future and realize
your most desired dreams*

1.13

CITADEL UNDERGROUND

tales
of
Beatnik
Glory

(A Citadel
Underground
Original)

Ed Sanders

"This irresistible book's droll charm leads the reader through a generation's coming-of-age."
—WILLIAM S. BURROUGHS

1.14

Johnny Got His Gun

1

2

2

3

4

5

6

7

7

CITADEL UNDERGROUND

Dalton Trumbo

With a new introduction by Ron Kovic

$1.15

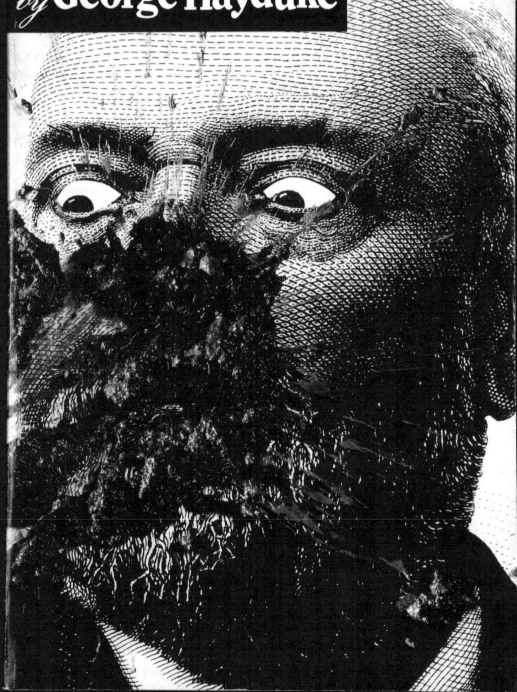

Advanced Backstabbing *and* Mudslinging Techniques *by* George Hayduke

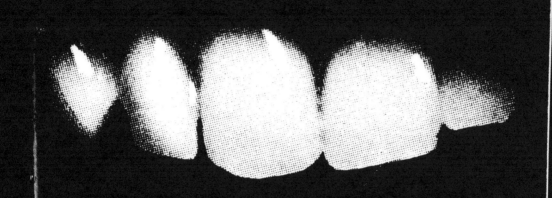

The Werewolf of Paris
Guy Endore

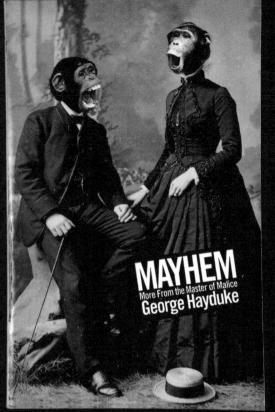

1.18

The Secrets of
Love Magick

*How to attract a lover, make
a former lover return to you...
and much, much more*
Gerina Dunwich
Author of Candlelight Spells

1.19

Erje Ayden
Foreword by Seymour Krim Preface by Frank O'Hara

1.20

1.21

Hélène Cixoys

Three Steps
on the Ladder
of Writing

"Hélène Cixous is today, in
my view, the greatest writer
in what I will call my language,
the French language if you
like. And I am weighing my
words as I say that. For a great
writer must be a poet-thinker,
very much a poet and a very
thinking poet."
—Jacques Derrida,
introducing the second of Cixous's
1990 Wellek Library lectures

1.22

Guernica
and Other Plays
FERNANDO ARRABAL

1.23

Gilles Deleuze
and Félix Guattari
The authors of ANTI-OEDIPUS

What Is
Philos-
ophy?

1.24

mea
cuba

An enduringly
original literary presence,
unquestionably Cuba's most
important living writer.
—Alastair Reid, The New York
Review of Books

Guillermo Cabrera Infante
Translated by KENNETH HALL with the author

1.25

VICTORE DESIGN WORKS
146 East 46th Street
New York, NY 10017 USA
tel 212.682.3734
fax 212.682.2921
Open 23 Hours

2

2. Early Promotional Cards

I was constantly looking for new freelance work, or even (perish the thought!) a steady job. By my late twenties I had compiled a list of rejection letters from some of the industry's finest designers. *C'est la guerre.* I was pretty good at making cold calls and humping my portfolio through the streets, but I was very good at getting weekly and monthly self-promotional material out the door to potential clients and studios. These promo cards were collaged, Xeroxed, hand painted—sometimes all at once. Later, it became clear to me that they were the basis for what would eventually become a style, borrowing simultaneously from two seemingly incongruous sources: design (modernism) and painting (expressionism). Bold and centered, with no subtlety. Strong, unpolished, and—hopefully— irreverent, funny, and brave.

My inspiration for this type of courageous work was Henryk Tomaszewski (1914–2005). Widely considered the father of the modern poster, Tomaszewski was one of the designers I vividly remembered from the books I had seen at the university library. There was something so completely free about his work. It employed none of the rules or grids I had heard of in design school—and certainly none of the typography I was supposed to have learned. It came, instead, out of a painterly or emotional approach. Whittling each idea down to its purest, most polished, and essential elements, Tomaszewski arrived at deceptively simple images— but within that simplicity resided wit, energy, and layers of meaning.

3. Greeting Cards

For four years I designed greeting cards for a company called Rohnart. It sounds like a straightforward enough endeavor: Design cute holiday and greeting cards, like Hallmark's, with sappy, endearing messages devoid of any emotion or meaning. I worked freelance and on commission, which meant the more cards I created, the more I got paid. The challenge was to come up with as many ideas as possible on the simple themes of "Happy Mother's Day," "Happy Father's Day," "Happy Easter," "Happy Bar Mitzvah," and so on. Every spring I was already in Christmas mode, creating hundreds of "Happy Holidays" designs in order to end up with a few new good ideas. Sketching became like the discipline of doing push-ups; in order to become strong you can't do three—you have to do twenty or fifty or a hundred. The process was this: Examine the cliché, then dig deeper into the idea, and do that again and again, turning and twisting it each time. Carving each idea down to a sharper and sharper point. As tedious as it sounds, this practice still forms my base, and is the core strength of my work. The hell with genius. Work hard.

FRAGILE

folds

①

②

happy Father's Day

my w
like a
Flane
Turned
Tupside down.
G. APOLLINARE

you are
here

3

servants…. With fifty men we could subjugate them all and make them do whatever we want."

—Christopher Columbus from *A People's History of the United States* by Howard Zinn

Racism

4. Celebrate Columbus

By 1992, most design studios were working on a Mac IIsi, or better yet, a new Quad. I was not as quick to respond to the technology craze. The only computer I had access to was one at my girlfriend's job. I would sit there, after hours, chasing little boxes of type around a small screen. This proved little fun. I preferred, and still prefer, working with my hands. I'd use scissors, paint, and preseparated mechanicals that I sent off to the printer complete with hand-drawn crop marks and layers of vellum and tissue, all held down to a Bainbridge board with wax, white tape, and the occasional cat hair (Figure 4.1).

I had moved to New York to become a poster designer, not knowing this position didn't exist as a paying gig. It still doesn't. But in my youthful idealism I was a believer. I felt I was privileged to be working in the design field. I thought graphic design was the most important work in the world. And I wanted to make work that was dangerous; otherwise it was not worth doing. But the truth was, I was making book jackets, not posters. These were not terribly dangerous. And I was being art directed, sometimes heavily.

In the fall of '92 I read an article in the *New York Times* about the celebrations New York City had planned for the five hundredth anniversary of Christopher Columbus's discovery of America. Now, I am no expert on Christopher Columbus or Native American history; what I know is what I remember from grade school: The Indians met Columbus, Pocahontas saved John Smith, then they all had Thanksgiving. But now some questions were raised. Where were the Indians today? What had they been doing? Why did I not know any? I felt the need to add to the conversation. What about the pox-infected blankets? What about the genocide? I knew the odds of the *New York Times* printing a satirical letter in strong opposition to the festivities were low.

And I also knew that the freedom of the press belongs to those who own a press.

So I turned to print. No sketches, no client, and no money, except for what was earmarked for rent. I pressed on regardless, paid the printer as well as the "official" company that hangs posters throughout New York "Post No Bills" City. Thus began my obsession with posters. And a had business plan.

Social responsibility is the duty of anyone who gives a damn.

In the fall of 1991 race riots broke out in Crown Heights, Brooklyn, when a Hasidic Jewish driver caused the injury of one black child and the death of another. When the driver stepped out of his station wagon, he was attacked by angry black bystanders, who beat and robbed him. This heightened the already existing tension in the racially mixed neighborhood.

For two years there were daily reports of "racism" in the press. The word was becoming ubiquitous and meaningless. I didn't want it to lose its ugly face. I set to work on a poster. It was hung in Brooklyn in early February 1993, the same week a car bomb exploded under the World Trade Center.

This is not limited to designers; we just happen to have the skills and tools at our side. In school, designers learn about Johannes Gutenberg and the invention of the printing press in the 1430s, but our fascination with technology blinds us to the next step in the process—the use of the press, coupled with an idea. In 1517, in Wittenberg, Saxony (Germany), Martin Luther nailed his Ninety-five Theses to the door of the All Saints' Church. In these documents, Luther openly criticized the church and the pope, calling them corrupt for, among other things, the practice of selling indulgences (freedom from God's punishment could be bought). And he called the pope a whore to boot.

The interesting part is in considering Martin Luther as an activist and graphic designer. Luther made use of the printing press to distribute his ideas through pamphlets, complete with illustrations (*The Whore of Babylon*) by his friend Lucas Cranach the Elder. Very quickly Luther's Theses were distributed and reprinted throughout Europe, thus beginning the Protestant Reformation. For this Luther was excommunicated from the church and proclaimed an outlaw by the state. Martin Luther himself wrote, "I would never have thought that such a storm would rise from Rome over one simple scrap of paper."

My point is oversimplified, but true. Through their commitment to an idea, the use of a press, and the bravery to hang and distribute their work, designers can engender profound change.

I was still an apprentice at the time in Paul Bacon's Carnegie Hall studio, a few blocks from Columbus Circle and ground zero for the big parade. Across the street was a construction site, where six of my Columbus posters were dutifully hung between Calvin Klein ads (featuring scantily clad teenage models frolicking in a faux wood-paneled basement) and posters for *Lethal Weapon 3*. While I was out one day admiring my work, two things happened that solidified my relationship with poster making. First, I saw people on the sidewalk stopping in front of my posters and reading them. Actually reading the damn things, even craning their necks sideways to study the fine print. I had made someone stop. A miracle—and something I was told in school would never happen. Second, the police came. They stopped as well, but not to read my posters. It was to scrape them off the wall with an old mop handle, being careful to leave the Calvin Klein posters unharmed. I was confused. Didn't I, too, pay for the right to be on the wall? Had I not used a commercial printer, sought the right format to print on, and followed the rules? I refrained from asking the cops these questions.

"Arawak men and women, naked, tawney, and full of wonder, emerged from their villages onto the island's beaches and swam out to get a closer look at the strange boat. When Columbus and his sailors came ashore, carrying swords, speaking oddly, the Arawaks ran to greet them, brought them food, water, gifts. He later wrote in his log: They...brought us parrots and balls of cotton and spears and many other things, which they exchanged for the glass beads and hawk's bells. They willingly traded everything they owned.... They were well-built, with good bodies and handsome features.... They do not bear arms, and do not know them, for I showed them a sword, they took it by the edge and cut themselves out of ignorance. They have no iron. Their spears are made of cane.... They would make fine

Celebrate Columbus
1492-1992

F.P.O.

América hoy, 500 años después / America today, 500 years later / L'Amérique aujourd' hui, 500 ans plus tard

50% MECHANICAL

PANTONE
449U

1,500 PIECES

Celebrate Columbus
1492-1992

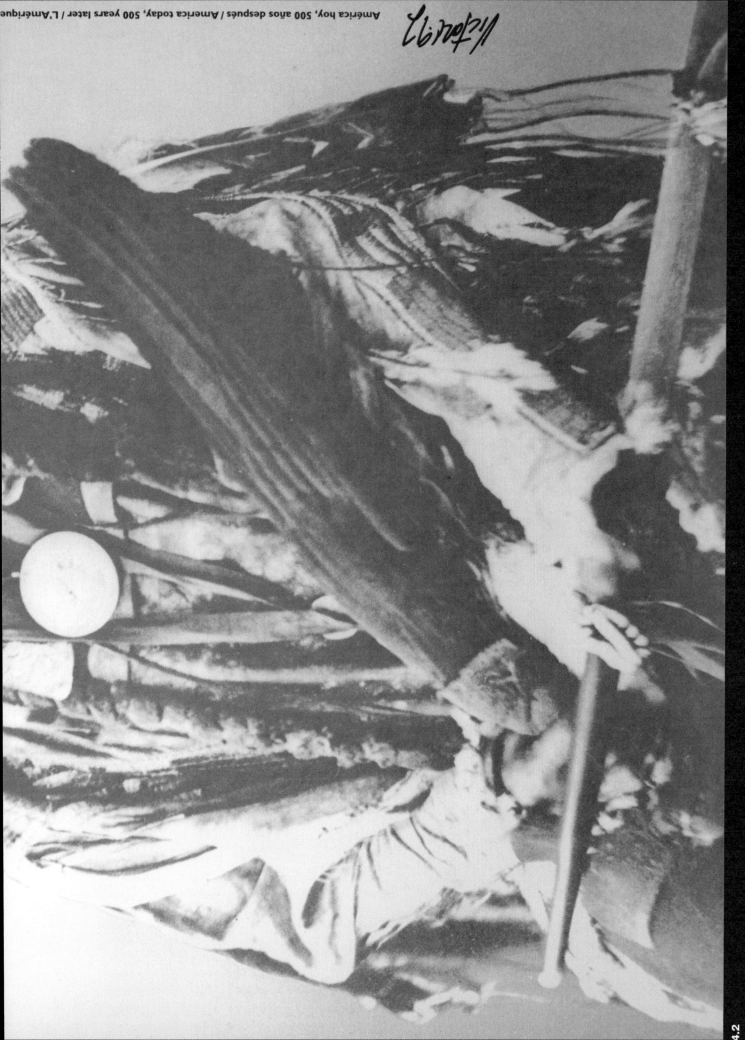

Racism and the Death Penalty

More than 200 years after the declaration that "all men are created equal," race still influences the American legal system. Racial bias affects criminal penalties and sentences, creating separate and unequal justice. The Capital Punishment Projects of the ACLU and the NAACP LDF have released a new video to educate the public about the death penalty and the need for a fairer criminal justice system. For more information, call the ACLU at 202.675.2321 or the NAACP LDF at 212.219.1900. "Double Justice" A documentary film about race and the death penalty.

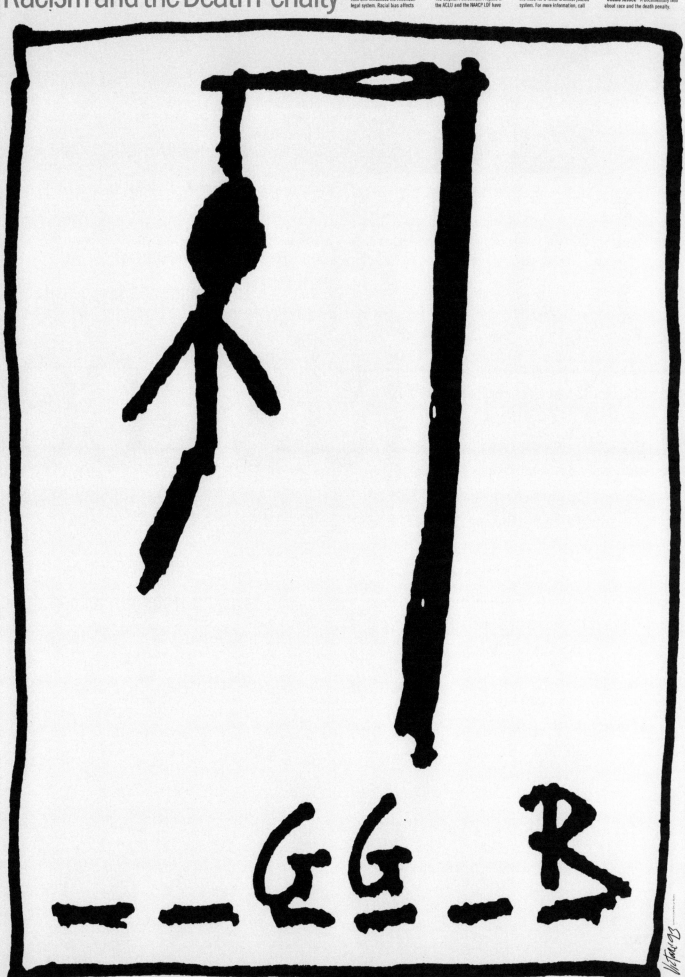

all men are created equal

THE GETTYSBURG ADDRESS

Racism and the Death Penalty

Over 200 years ago, the Declaration of Independence proclaimed that "all men are created equal." Yet from the very inception of the United States, Americans have been unequal before the law.

The slave codes, enacted in the colonies in the 1700's to govern the conduct and treatment of African Americans and other peoples of color, established race as a basis for settling matters of crime and punishment.

Race still influences the way the American criminal justice system works, with the attitudes that once justified slavery continuing to produce a double standard today. The discriminatory consequences of that double standard are nowhere more stark than in the application of the death penalty.

While many Americans of all colors may regard the death penalty as a legitimate means of eliminating individuals who threaten their lives and property, few are aware that our legal system places a premium on the lives of white people. In some states, race is apparently the single most important factor in determining who will be sentenced to die and who will

double justice

"Double Justice" combines historical information about the racially biased use of the death penalty with contemporary research that demonstrates the continuing impact of race, particularly the race of crime victims, in determining whether a death sentence will be imposed. A moving visual commentary highlighted by the magic of computer animation, "Double Justice" takes information that for too long has been confined to scholarly works, law books and legal briefs and makes it accessible to the general public.

be spared that ultimate punishment. In Georgia, for example, studies show that blacks accused of killing whites are 4 times more likely to receive the death penalty than whites accused of killing blacks. A 1991 report produced by the Chattahoochee Judicial Circuit of Georgia reveals a clear pattern in the way death sentences are meted out in the state: Crimes against white victims are treated as inherently more serious than crimes against non-whites. The consequences of this pattern are devastating for African-Americans, whom the criminal justice system often treats with indifference, or worse, contempt.

Nationwide, those accused of crimes against white victims are more likely to receive a death sentence than a prison term compared to those whose victims are black. In February 1990, the General Accounting Office, the investigative arm of Congress, reviewed more than 28 studies and confirmed the existence of *a pattern of evidence indicating racial disparities in the charging, sentencing and imposition of the death sentence.* These studies, spanning 15 years of death-sentencing in modern times, reflect a fundamental undervaluing of the lives of African American victims and capital defendants that amounts to a double standard of justice.

The ACLU Capital Punishment Project and the NAACP LDF are committed to aggressive new methods of educating the public about race and the death penalty. While the traditional debate format can be useful in raising public awareness about the issues, too often the timing and setting of debates are not optimum for achieving large-scale public rejection of capital punishment. Videos provide a unique opportunity to educate both large and targeted segments of the public under ideal conditions.

"Double Justice" combines historical information about the racially biased use of the death penalty with contemporary research that demonstrates the continuing impact of race, particularly the race of the victim, in determining whether a death sentence will be imposed.

For the last three decades, the NAACP LDF and the ACLU have been working to bring about abolition of the death penalty and protecting the constitutional rights of death row inmates. While much of this work has historically taken place in the federal courts, federal litigation on behalf of death row inmates has reached a crisis stage. In addition, the criminal justice policies of the past 12 years have had a devastating impact on communities of color. "Double Justice" is a crucial tool in the effort to mobilize public opinion *against* the death penalty and *for* a more equitable system of criminal justice.

Capital Punishment

"The impact of our heritage of slave laws will continue to make itself felt into the future. For there is a nexus between the brutal centuries of colonial slavery and the racial polarization and anxieties of today. The poisonous legacy of legalized oppression based upon the matter of color can never be adequately purged from our society if we act as if it had never existed." —A. Leon Higginbotham, Jr. *Chief Emeritus of the United States Court of Appeals for the Third Circuit*

LDF ACLU

NAACP Legal Defense and Educational Fund, Inc. Capital Punishment Project 99 Hudson Street Suite 1600 New York, NY 10013-2897 212-219-1900 fax 212-226-7592
American Civil Liberties Union Capital Punishment Project 122 Maryland Avenue NE Washington, DC 20002 202-675-2331 fax 202-546-0738

"Double Justice" was made possible by generous financial support from the J. Roderick MacArthur Foundation.
"Double Justice" Videotape 19 minutes $29.95 Producers/Directors: Diana Rose Fortuna, Executive, ACLU Capital Punishment Project; Katiana Wicks, Katiana Visuals/Reynolds Printing, NAACP Legal Defense and Educational Fund, Inc.
Project Manager: John Mitzewich, Kevin Everson Producers of "American Drug Fortune," National Public Radio and public television. Video Peace: Alice Ferguson, Designer, Advanced Visualization/Associate Professor of Communications, NYU
Webb Company, Barron Valley College, N.J. All this must be prepared hard water and mirrors, accompanied by a kaleidoscopic video palette to the American Civil Liberties Union, to ACLU Departments 1, P.O. Box 794, Medford, NY 11763
All parties should be directed to the NAACP Legal Defense and Educational Fund, Inc. or the American Civil Liberties Union or the above affiliation.
Contributions to that organization's work to advance a society that fulfills the Constitution's promise of equality and justice are tax-deductible.
Printed in the U.S.A.

6. Double Justice

In 1993 the NAACP commissioned the film *Double Justice*, documenting the racism inherent in the application of the death penalty, and I was asked to create a poster for it. Only five hundred copies of the film were being distributed, but the budget allowed for printing fifteen hundred copies of the poster. The posters were not meant to be hung in the street, but were sent directly to educators, lawmakers, lobbyists, lawyers, and teachers throughout Washington, DC. The reverse side featured text from the film and additional information on the application of the death penalty, so the poster could be used as an educational tool on its own (Figure 6.2).

Generally speaking, not-for-profit groups tend to shy away from too much truth telling. The direct approach is put aside in the interest of presenting more aesthetically appealing "advertising." Understandable, since they largely rely on donations from happy constituents; boat rocking (or truth telling) is not as profitable. The only reason this poster, with its extremely bold message, saw the light of day was sheer speed. We were at the printer just fourteen days after our initial meeting. No one at the NAACP had time to overanalyze the idea or get over their initial excitement or shock.

I am sometimes surprised when my work "grows legs" and takes on a life of its own. In February 1994, just after he reversed his opinion on the death penalty, Supreme Court Justice Harry Blackmun (author of Roe v. Wade) called the NAACP to obtain copies of the hangman poster. It can still be found on the walls of various government offices throughout the capitol.

The way the puzzle is "read" is something I have always found very interesting. There is no surface evidence that the subject is black Americans, and there are at least sixteen common words in the English language that solve this puzzle, yet the first word that comes to mind is always *nigger*.

7. The Shakespeare Project

"Evolved individuals know that peo-ple who are not intuitive can be dangerous to work with, since they are guided by the current appear-ance of things that are in reality, changing." —Lao Tzu, *Tao Te Ching*

I was a regular at Berry's, a local bar in SoHo where Scott Cargle, an ac-tor, was bartender. Scott wasn't interested in the kind of work available to hungry young actors, mainly television commercials and cameos on soaps; he wanted to do Shakespeare—real theater. He wanted to act with the same purpose, creativity, and freedom with which I wanted to design. He also happened to be very good at paperwork and administration.

Recognizing our common interests, we joined forces and created a not-for-profit organization called the Shakespeare Project. Our collective goal was to bring full-length Shakespeare plays to New Yorkers free of charge, outdoors. (As vice president and design director, I became my own client—something akin to the uncomfortable position of onanism.) Starting in 1993 with a budget of $350, we set out to do a production of *Romeo and Juliet*. Because of the nature of these performances, I was freed from putting any ancillary information on the posters. Actors were not paid, and changed frequently, so their names were not put down in print. Per-formance venues and dates often changed because of weather, so that information wasn't included, either. Similar to the techniques employed by the traveling circus, I left space at the bottom of the poster to write in:

TODAY!   TOMPKINS   FREE
3PM!!   SQUARE
    PARK!!

Next, we began customizing our audience to our performances. We staged *The Taming of the Shrew*—essentially a story of spousal abuse—for a rapt audience at a women's shelter. By 2000 we had, thanks to Scott's excellent business savvy and unending energy, a budget of eighty thou-sand dollars to perform *Venus and Adonis*, one of Shakespeare's poems converted into a play. *Venus and Adonis* was one of the Bard's bestselling works until the Victorian age, when it was deemed too lewd. This curse was to befall our little band of players, too, and would mark the end of my relationship with the Project. I presented an initial image for the poster (something about animals having sex) that was killed before the play ran because Con Ed would pull their $20K of funding if we ran the "questionable" image. We had sold our freedom. Our sponsor had become art director. I came up with an alternate solution (the bunny), then fired the Shakespeare Project.

FREE

Twelfth Night

The Shakespeare Project *presents* Twelfth Night *or What You Will,* by Wm. Shakespeare. Admission is Free *Directed by* Scott Cargle. Our performances are; Central Park, Saturday June 11 at 12:00 PM and 4 PM. Sunday June 12 at 3:00 PM. Bryant Park, Sunday, June 19 and 26 at 3:00 PM. Fort Green Park, Brooklyn, Saturday, June 18 at 12:00 PM and 4:00 PM., and at The Henry Street Settlement, Abrons Art Center, Thursday, June 16 at 6:00 PM. Donations are greatly appreciated.

THE SHAKESPEARE PROJECT *presents*

ROMEO JULIET

7.4

THE SHAKESPEARE PROJECT *presents* William Shakespeare's

CORIOLANUS

THE SHAKESPEARE PROJECT *presents*

MACBETH

8. Traditional Family Values

At the 1992 Republican National Convention in Houston, Patrick Buchanan gave the keynote address—his famous "culture war" speech, in which he first uttered the words *traditional family values*. By this he meant a return to the opiate state of nostalgia, the kind of Americana stereotyped by church and family, without the nasty bits of multiculturalism, abortion, or gay rights.

After the convention, political columnist and humorist Molly Ivins wrote in the *Dallas Times Herald* that Buchanan's speech "probably sounded better in the original German."

9. The Death Penalty Mocks Justice

In my newfound zeal to change the world, I took on a second project for the NAACP Legal Defense and Educational Fund. This one dealt with the United States being the only "first world" or "civilized" country to still employ capital punishment. Initially the project was meant to be a two-sided informational poster like Double Justice, but delays in the writing and editing of the back-side text left the project budget leaking onto the floor. We decided to run to the printer with the small amount of finished text on the front of the poster. Done is better than perfect.

Traditional Family Values!

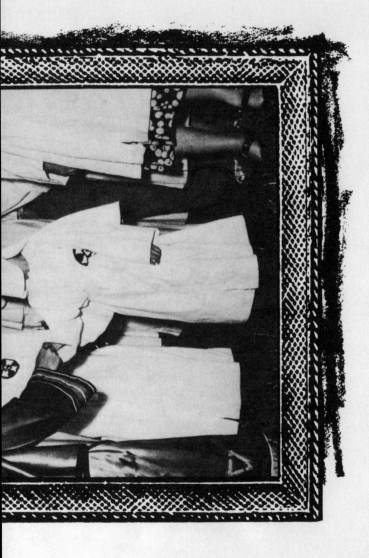

The Death Penalty Mocks Justice

The United States remains the only Western industrialized nation to retain the death penalty and carry out executions. While the rest of the world turns its back on state sanctioned killing, the death penalty in the U.S. continues to be applied in a racist and arbitrary manner. Capital punishment has never been implemented in a fair and non-discriminatory way. It has never been proven to be a deterrent, yet our nations death row, and executions continue to escalate. The death penalty is a mockery of justice. In the pursuit of equality before the law it must be abolished.

NAACP Legal Defense and Educational Fund, Inc. Capital Punishment Project
99 Hudson Street Suite 1600 New York, NY 10013-2897 tel. 212.219.1900 fax 212.226.7592
Contributions to the NAACP LDF work to achieve a society that fulfills the Constitution's
promise of equality and justice and are tax deductible.

10. Do Not Feed the Animals

This project happened completely backassward. The poster was created as a counter to Mayor Rudy Giuliani's fascist campaign to clean up New York City at any cost, by removing street vendors, graffiti, and the homeless. My specific target was a poster issued by the Metropolitan Transportation Authority of New York that asked subway passengers to give their monies to official charities and not directly to homeless persons (Figure 10.1). Their poster was not only ill-conceived, in that it attempted to tell you what to think when you sat in front of it—an Orwellian feature that probably made Giuliani drool—but it was also just butt-ugly. In order to make my own poster "official," I put the MTA logo and the mayor's name in the lower corner.

After paying to print it, I realized I had to get someone else to pay to hang it, and approached New York City's Coalition for the Homeless. The poster was hung throughout the city. And since it carried the seal of the mayor's office and the MTA logo, it was very properly hung next to the subway entrances.

I sat back and waited for a SWAT team to kick down my door, but they never came.

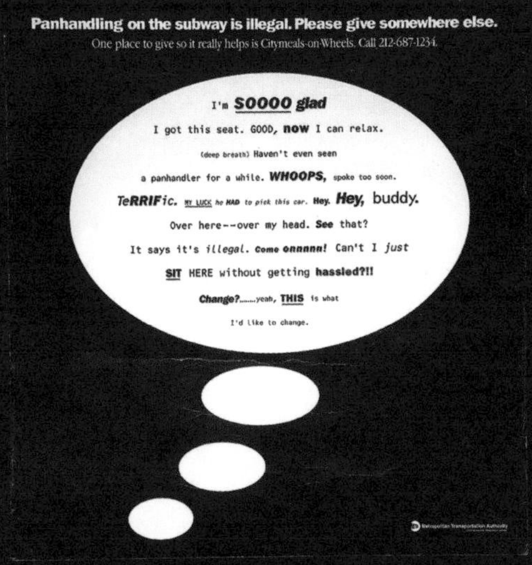

10.1

**DO NOT FEED
THE ANIMALS**

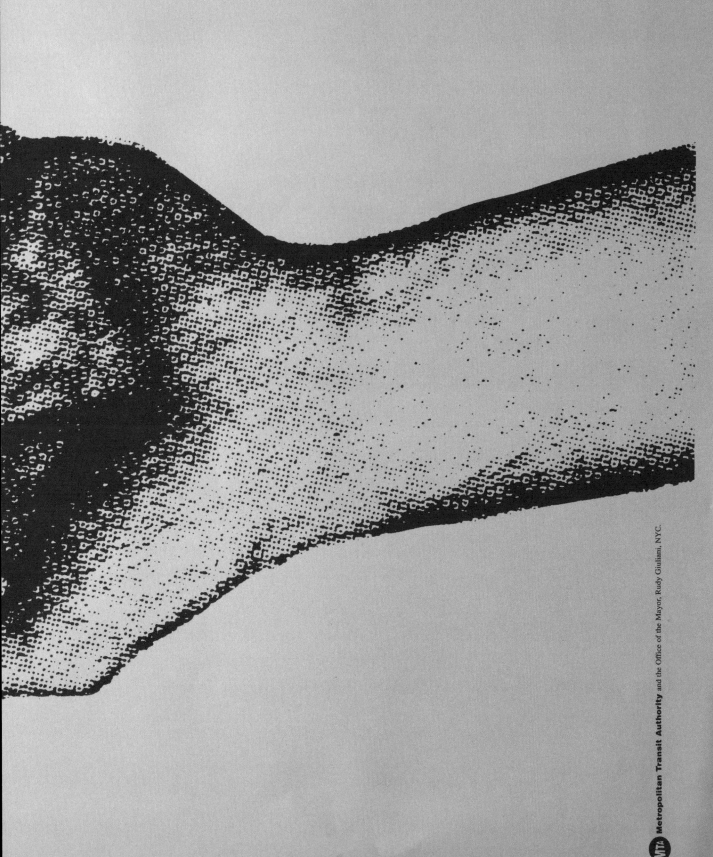

10.2

10.3

11. Fair Game in America

The March/April 1999 issue of *Mother Jones* magazine was titled "In Your Face Protest." Along with a handful of other designers, I was given a page of the magazine on which to create an imaginary poster (which was never reproduced as an actual poster) on any topic I felt close to. Being a dilettante allows me to feel close to a number of topics at the same time, but one issue I have always felt strongly about is the availability and easy access to handguns and assault weapons in the United States. The month the magazine came out, two heavily armed young men walked into their high school in Columbine, Colorado, and opened fire, killing twelve students and a teacher.

Fair Game _ in America

12.1

The art in my parents' house played a great role in my development. My father was an amateur photographer. Being in the Air Force, he photographed clouds and airplanes. We had the requisite copy of Norman Rockwell's collected works, which I pored over often, a reproduction of Toulouse-Lautrec's *Moulin Rouge* poster that I saw every day, a large collection of Maxfield Parrish prints, Spanish bullfight posters from my father's travels, as well as antiques and exotics from around the world. This early introduction to art and design, and the crossover of the two—artists creating magazine covers, painters making posters—along with my father's international travels, laid the seeds for my interest not only in art and design but in what lay outside my hometown.

It made perfect sense, then, that acceptance of my work came from abroad before it came from home (my first solo exhibition was in Osaka, Japan, Figure 12.1). Poster Love announces a Prague gallery exhibition of work by myself and two poster-designer friends, Karel Misek, from the Czech Republic, and Kari Pippo, from Finland. It is a much more "European" view that what we as designers make could be considered art. I have been blessed and lucky to have had the opportunity to travel the world, both to exhibit my work and to lecture about it. Besides providing direct contact with a helpful and critical public, the experience has forced on me a level of introspection and self-reflection, hopefully improving my work—or at least my attitude toward it.

Poster Love
Karel Miśek Karl Pippo James Victore

Critique ®

THE
MAGAZINE
OF
GRAPHIC
DESIGN
THINKING

~~$22~~ $18

Simplify, simplify.

—THOREAU

13

The

Art

xt
that
ity
an
re.
ors,
th.

DANCE

of
ECONOMY

IS NOTHING MORE THAN

A Big

VICTORE

SQUEEZED
THROUGH

A

Small
Budget

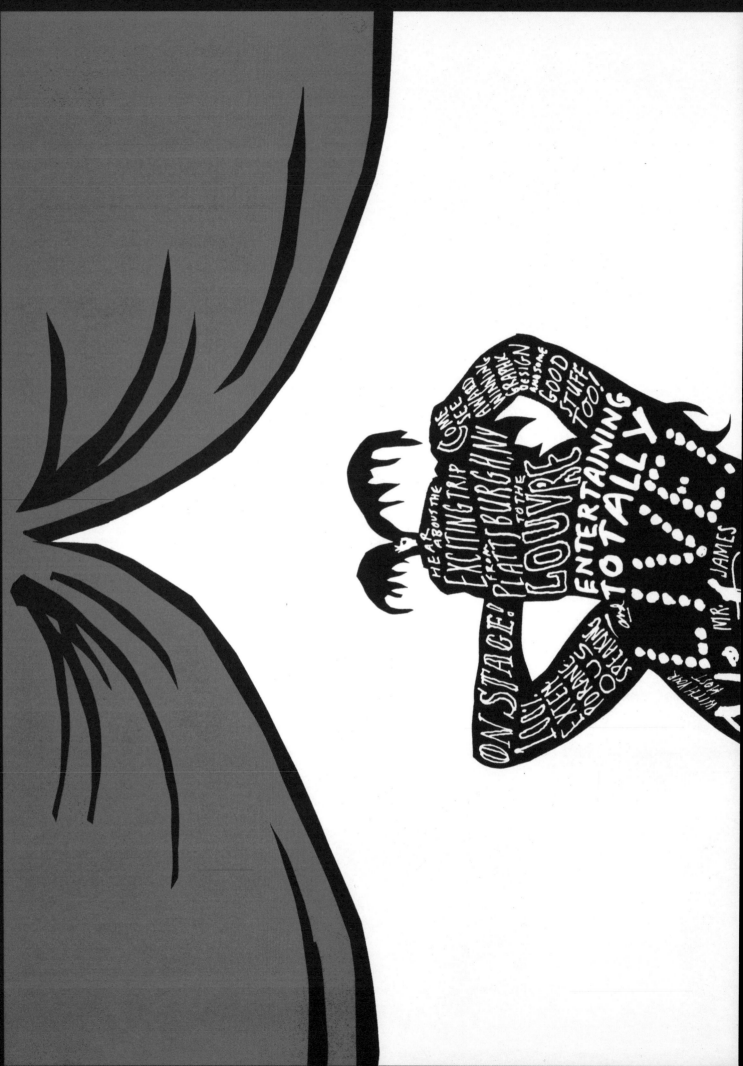

14

13. Critique

Thoreau was a windbag.

14. Totally Live

One of my first speaking engagements was at the State University of New York at Plattsburgh, the (first) university I failed out of. Thanks to the efforts of my mother, who worked at the university library, SUNY hosted me, and agreed to print posters for the talk. When I arrived, however, there wasn't a poster in sight. I was a bit perplexed, considering their efforts and the cost of printing. When I inquired into the matter, I learned that the posters had been twice put up, and were twice stolen by the students—the ultimate compliment.

I had made something that people wanted to steal.

This had always been my goal.

15. Use a Condom

Seriously, use one.

16. Animation

I don't concern myself terribly about "what the public wants," or even "what the client wants." If we try to please everybody, our attempts always funnel down to some phony Beatlemania and we can never be free to create anything new. If I can surprise myself, then I may be in a position to surprise others.

Working in television animation proved to me the power that two guys fooling around can have. My friend Brian Hall was the creative director for WVIT TV in Hartford, Connecticut. We were out drinking together and looking at some of my sketches for greeting cards when Brian casually suggested that they would look good animated. So we did it; we created two fifteen-second station-identification spots, both hand-done cel animation, one for Halloween and one for the winter holidays. We did it over some pasta and Chianti. We allowed ourselves complete freedom—and were later awarded an Emmy and a Broadcast Designers Association gold and silver medal for the effort.

"Do what you feel in your heart to be right—for you'll be criticized anyway. You'll be damned if you do, and damned if you don't."
—Eleanor Roosevelt

16.2

16.3

17. Portfolio Center

Small is beautiful. For almost fifteen years, I have had a client that continually pushes me and my work. They are strong and brave, and they pay me in American money. The Portfolio Center in Atlanta, Georgia, is a mom-and-pop school for advertising, design, and the related arts, a place full of love, attention, and consistency—hard to find in a school environment. We have grown together. They've allowed me the freedom to experiment and have had the sense to pull me back when I've gone too far. I've worked with the boss. No committees. Approvals have come from the president. We've shared a "live by the sword, die by the sword" attitude. We've taken chances. Some were successful; others, less so, but we were willing to live with that.

One particular case was a full-page advert we created titled "Shinola (Figure 17.8)," as in the Southern phrase that roughly translates as "doesn't know bad from good." Presumably, the school would take you from unknowing to knowing. Our hubris was a bit much for the design community, and they wrote letters to prove it (Figure 17.9). Even the student body was split into pro- and contra-"Shinola" factions. At a speaking engagement at the school, one of the advertising majors asked, "Mr.

Victore, are you telling me that you are willing to take the school's money and make advertising that may not work?" My answer was, "Yes. This is what I am paid to do."

If I worked with a safety net, it would be less interesting. There are no guarantees in what designers do. If you want something close to a guarantee, you can hedge your bets and hire a focus group, or, better yet, ask your mom.

Over time we created an identity for the school—a look and feel. It wasn't a cookie-cutter style or a rubber-stamp logo, but an overall visual feel that soon became easy to recognize. When placing ads in magazines, I wanted to make the most beautiful, ugly, or even confounding pages in them. Every catalogue we made was made to be a gift. When it showed up in your mailbox, you knew you were holding something special—holding energy. After a recent workshop, a young designer told me she has moved three times since finishing school and still keeps her old Portfolio Center catalogue. Fuck recycling; just make things that folks don't throw away.

My wish for every designer is that they be lucky enough, at least once in their career, to have a client like this. That they have the opportunity to be on the winning end of compromise, and get a taste of what the designer-client relationship should be. It will likely ruin them for all the others.

ART TES

To the Teit are five pair of designs. Study each design pair. Place ai cher mark under a ther design that best ya lustrates meaning if the word low it. Ch only one to in each lof the five pairs.

Art Instruction
Use the comp
ducl of the stud
To sem. or you
has good al

☐ Tired?
☐ Outcast?
☐ Restless?
☐ See things differently?
☐ Want more out of life...

Tell us about you
The information you
fel to us is helping
over each question
for___

"Draw Me"
Sketch a famous Draw
Draw the head of

CHANGE

17.1

PoRTfolio CEnter

CHANGE "Would you

START HERE.

Sometime in your life, someone has looked at something you've written, drawn or photographed, and said, "Wow, you really should do something with your talent. I wish I could be half that talented." And you thought, Oh yeah, smart guy? Well, what would you do with half the talent? Would you draw the little pirate and trundle off to art school so you could learn to do drawings for your local church bulletin? Maybe you would send your photographs to some local whatzit who would publish your blood-felt work in a mindless zine that's dust and forgotten before the ink dries. Maybe, you would score a matte room job at a local ad or design firm, brewing coffee and cutting and pasting for the *Real Creatives*. And by the time you turned 65, your career would just be taking off with your heart clogging up from years of stress and cheap food. Maybe. That's the back atcha inside your head for those people who so admire your talent. But also in your head you're thinking, wondering, worrying that your talent might be some sort of cosmic joke or self-delusion. Maybe you're merely a worm. Or maybe, yes maybe, you're a caterpillar, and, given the time and the proper environment, not only could you make *something* of your life, but something beautiful and purposeful.

READY?

A TEST

Kevin Bacon is six degrees away from everybody. If he'd gone to Portfolio Center he'd only be about a degree-and-a-half away from just about anybody who's anybody in the world of Advertising, Graphic Design and Media Architecture, Illustration and Photography. Two years from now you might be jetting off to California. That is, after all, how this adventure ends. You score the big job and find yourself travelling the world doing cool work for cool people. Those become your big years once you complete the change of life that is your Portfolio Center experience. But how do you get from here to there? How do you convert your drop-person marketing campaign on behalf of your own favorite charity? What's the coolest stuff that gets you the killer job? Well, to get there, whether there is California or Frankfurt, you'll find yourself accessing an unmatched network of people in the communication arts. **CAREER DEVELOPMENT** And it starts here, at school, with the office. Your own personal industry research, a pursuit you begin when you arrive at PC, coupled with the industry and graduate databases in the CD office, will transform you into a job-seeking, name-taking, creative cyborg. Ruthlessly efficient. And that, my friend, is the mysterious stuff that gets you there. The next thing you know, you're there, which is some little bistro in Paris. And it turns out that the director of your shoot plays backgammon for money with a close personal friend of the ex-brother-in-law of the pet groomer who does the curls of long-haired dachshund that belongs to a supermodel who has paintball battles with (you guessed it) Kevin Bacon.

ILLUSTRATION

But does Portfolio Center really work? And will it help me get rid of unwanted hair? Just read these testimonials from ACTUAL PC GRADS!

This Stuff You Just Can't Make Up...
Strange Yet True Tales of Change

LOOK WHAT'S HAPPENING FOR PEOPLE WHO ATTEND PORTFOLIO CENTER!

You've been closed a long time now.

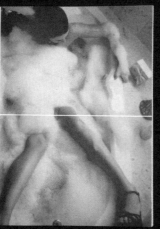

1.

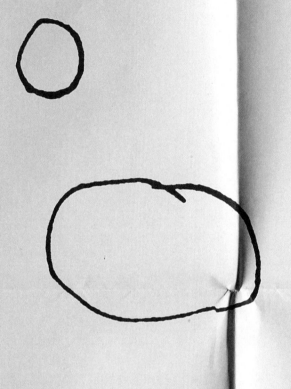

2.

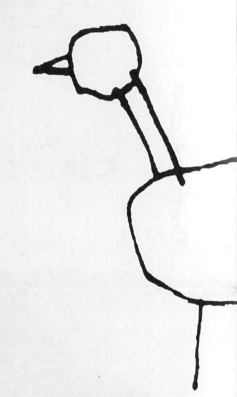

How to draw

3.

w a chicken.

How to find the newest talent.
tfolio Center Graduation and Review

ding off the newest talents to graduate from Portfolio Center. You will have an opportunity to review books and move about
howcasing themselves and their portfolios on March 25th from 9AM until 4PM. Before you leave you will be able to select candidates to interview the following day.
your leisure. Allow 2 to 3 hours to see all of the portfolios. You'll be able to meet with your selected candidates in small
th interviews will be scheduled in thirty-minute increments from 9AM to 4PM. We will make every effort to accommodate you. On the evening
meetings. If you have special support requests, audio-visual equipment for example, the accomplishments of our newest graduates. If you are
h at 7:30PM, family and friends are cordially invited to celebrate with staff and faculty Please RSVP for Portfolio Review with Claire Kerby at Portfolio Center
r reservations, plan for the ceremony to end around 10:00 PM.
9, ext.19 or e-mail us at Plcdev@portfoliocenter.com

James Victore

PortfolioCenter

Portfolio Center
125 Bennett Street, Atlanta, GA 30309 / 1.800.255.3169 / www.portfoliocenter.com
Live to Learn

PORTFOLIO
CENTER

CATALOG

THE End

THE End

17.6

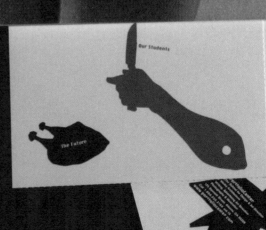

PortfolioCenter

x as TV and the Internet come
president/general manager
ghts with *Ad Age* from his three
tomized opportunities for
silk. "Advanced" TV ads and
interactive overlays during
text message opt-in requests,
length music video for Axe
huge viral success. It became
the on-demand Music
million hits on YouTube.[11]

George said, "and iTV is in 70
re accountability expands the
room and provides a way to
es that Unilever can't other-
important—why waste your
interested in it? The reach is
iewers spend between 2 and 14
TV. The goal to create
out rather than trying to stick

vertising agencies was made
an of NBC Sports. In August
adband access's influence on
ercials at the beginning of
ds would never for the kind
m Olympic broadcasters. We
digital pennies [13]

ly '60s, graphic designers were
thought of as a rified practice
institutions that they and
ink have nothing to do with
cording to Steven Heller. Lou
erb Lubalin and George Lois,
vertising designe presented by
as graphic design leaders who
.[15] He credits advertising design
gn. In contrast, Wilburn Bonnell
activity (how he refers to graphic
'60s as a profession separate and
design, and that the quartet of
and Dreyfuss were responsible for
ss that the look their products
was then just a small step to
of their companies could affect

phic design evolution did run
ution in advertising design. Many
os of 3–15 people concentrated

Letter to the editor,

Communication Arts, May/June 1997

Dear Editor,

Im writing to tell you my reaction to the full-page, full-color advertisement for The Portfolio Center appearing in the January/February issue on page 151. If the best this advertiser can tell me is that they can teach students how to tell shit from Shinola, it will be a long, long time before I will agree to review a portfolio from their organization. And I will never recommend The Portfolio Center as a place to learn the skills, talents and qualities required for success in our industry.

A key quality for success is, of course, good taste. It is not, however, the lack of good taste in this advertisement (the ad is such an incredible example of bad taste that it's repulsive to use the word *taste* at all) that I find so offensive. What I find offensive is its rank amateurism. Gross mindlessness of this sort is to be expected of pre-adolescent boys. As is to underscore the point, the ad was even turned sideways, a device that has been suggested to me, in my long career, by only the dumbest of advertisers.

I'm embarrassed that a publication which stands for the advancement of the highest quality in the creation and execution of marketing communication would stand for this advertisement appearing in its pages.

Glenn Ossiander
Bethlehem, Pennsylvania

Reply

Dear Editor,

I too am outraged. Outraged that not only did the ad that I designed for the Portfolio Center receive a "nasty letter" (May/June), but that there were two additional letters that found something "offensive" within the pages of CA, including RJ Muna's beautiful cover photograph. I am saddened and outraged that the design business is being bludgeoned to death by lackluster and humorless puritans.

I have no need to defend Portfolio Center for placing the ad, they not only do a remarkable job of turning out students with Shinola portfolios (who should stay the heck out of Mr. Ossiander's studio), but they do it fearlessly. I also applaud CA for running the ad and not patently and flippantly censoring it because "it won't fly in Bethlehem, PA." "Success in our industry", to quote Mrs. Ossiander, does not come from cautious, watered-down ideas, but from the playful, quirky and sometimes dangerous ones.

Love,
James Victore

18. Steven Heller

Steven Heller is the hardest-working man in the graphic design business. His ability to create opportunities for others is something that I envy.

My relationship with Steve began through the mail. He had written an article in one of the design magazines about the designer Lucian Bernhard, one of my personal favorites. I answered his article with a query, to which he was generous enough to respond. This modest exchange proved the beginning of a long and trusting relationship (now turned mentorship). Together we have designed what seems like an entire library of books on design—over twelve years, twenty-eight books and covers. And counting.

Design Literacy *Second Edition* — Heller

Marketing Illustration Heller and Marshall

The Education of an Illustrator — HELLER / ARTSMAN

Design Disasters: *Great Designers, Fabulous Failures & Lessons Learned* — Heller

Graphic Design Time Line

GRAPHIC DESIGN HISTORY Heller and Ballance

Inside the Business of Illustration Heller and Arisman

Letterforms *Bawdy Bad & Beautiful* Heller and Thompson

GENIUS MOVES Heller and Ilić

Texts on Type Heller and Meggs

SEX APPEAL *The Art of Allure in Graphic and Advertising Design* Steven Heller

18.1

Heller **The Education of a Typographer**

Less Is More Heller and Fink

Heller **Design Humor:** The Art of Graphic Wit

Teaching Illustration Edited by Steven Heller and Marshall Arisman

DESIGN LITERACY

Heller **TEACHING GRAPHIC DESIGN** HELLER *and* POMEROY

The Education of a Comics Artist Dooley and Heller

Heller and Vienne **THE Education of an Art Director**

Steven HELLER **EDUCATION OF A DESIGN ENTREPRENEUR**

Design Literacy (continued) Steven Heller

Traub, Heller, and Bell **The Education of a Photographer**

Design Dialogues Heller and Pettit

Heller **The Education of a Graphic Designer/ Second Edition**

Heller **The Education of an E-Designer**

Heller & Vienne **Citizen Designer:** Perspectives on Design Responsibility

Desig
Disaste
Great Desi
Fabulo
Failur
& Lesse
Learni

Edited by Steven I

Section Four:
Sex, Power, Feminism

18.4

Less Is More

Less Is More Heller and Fink

The New Simplicity in Graphic Design

Steven Heller and Anne Fink

19. The New York Times

Drop everything you are doing for a $175, two-inch-square drawing that tomorrow will grace the floors of birdcages around the world!

I have never considered myself an "illustrator." The first instance where my work appeared with that attribution was on the op-ed page of the *New York Times*. Owing to a reference from Steve Heller, I served a short stint as art director of that section of the paper. In my role as the Grim Reaper of the illustration world, I once found myself in a pinch, with no one available during crunch time for one particular article. Not wanting to leave a gaping hole reading only

WITTY DRAWING GOES HERE

I filled the spot myself.

I have no other regular client with such topical content and access to a worldwide audience as the *Times*. The turnaround is quick—sometimes only few hours. This constraint brings a freshness and immediacy to the work. No time for fancy techniques or showmanship—just get to the core of the idea. I don't want too much time to "clean up" the work or second-guess myself anyway; it leaves too much room for self-doubt and fear to fester.

...ing

...ur

...ains

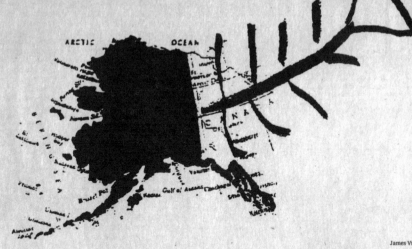

James Victore

WASHINGTON
...le agree that the
...ce the budget is to
...the relentless in-
...of Medicare.
...an of either party
...to the need to push
...st-saving managed
...benefits, or to ask
...substantial co-pay-

...r can we come up
...udgetary medicine
...eniors on Medicare
...ow can we replace
...pe?

...el laureates came
...week with a big
...er. One is the mo-
...James Watson, co-
...A; the other is the
...oper, pioneer of su-

...ters left their origi-
...concentrate on to-
...ng and productive
...the science of the

...and psychiatric dis-

Save Alaska — Again

By Jimmy Carter

ATLANTA

Alaska is America's last fron-
tier, home to our

vate native corporations and made
way for construction of the Trans-
Alaska oil pipeline. A second law —
one of my proudest accomplishments
as President — was the Alaska Lands
Act of 1980, which designated 104 mil...

The new Congress must be re-
awakened to the importance of protecting the interests of all Americans
by protecting public lands in Alaska.
For what is at stake is an unparal-
leled system of Federal reserves

...strong NATO
...he first piece of
...at NATO's bas-
...g the refugees
...e form of credi-
...ection — will be
...itting the alli-
...having suffered
...y and without a
...t beanbag.

...about is what
...ight to manage
...sovo Albanians
..., just as NATO
...Serbs, Croats
...nia. And why
...out that? Be-
...osnia. The Bos-
...an with a polit-
...een the leaders
...de facto parti-
...litary arrange-
...lt around that
...That is why it

...pposite. We are
...y arrangement
...political under-
...bs and Kosovo
...political future
...The Kosovo Al-
...independence;
...NATO out and
...y over Kosovo.
...O and Russia
...basically con-
...still-aggrieved
...w the U.S. and
...ng feud.
...e second bit of
...Milosevic will

...accord
...ovo
...ean.

...in some very

ing about not accepting foreign

Tim Judah is the author of "The
Serbs: History, Myth and the De-
struction of Yugoslavia."

since Mr. Milosevic thrives in such
circumstances, this is precisely why
we must not allow this to happen.
So the West must throw the Serbs
a lifeline. Even though led by an

fresh investment in Serbia, new jobs
and more money, this process of
rising expectations would have ac-
celerated.
There is another reason that Ser-

ed on Albanians in Kosovo is the im-
mediate challenge facing the international community. But, longer term,
Serbia must not be left isolated." We
ignore this advice at our peril. □

Bland word
can political
Politburo, wh
men massacr
officers who c
onage appar
appeasement
tries. Left out
Chinese and T
ularly those

Kil
mur
ou

expressing fo
The sardon
dent Clinton
would impr
rights and A
nasty joke by
the U.S.-Chin
their groupie
ment and pre
The engage
can nation. By
influence to
Communist p
U.S. unfaithfu
sustain Amer
Western m
propped up o
helps the Pol
dents, conde
labor and giv
between wors
controlled ch
for praying u
Another fo
utter passivi
nists to conti
against Tibe
knows Asia lo
the internatio
that only sha
zation are left
of imported c

South Africa's Lost Generation

Before   **After**

The New York Times Magazine

JUNE 18, 1995 / SECTION 6

ARE YOU MY FATHER?

Sperm donors were long anonymous.
But now kids are searching for their genetic kin,
and some donor dads even want to be found.
As if the modern family weren't complicated enough.

BY PEGGY ORENSTEIN

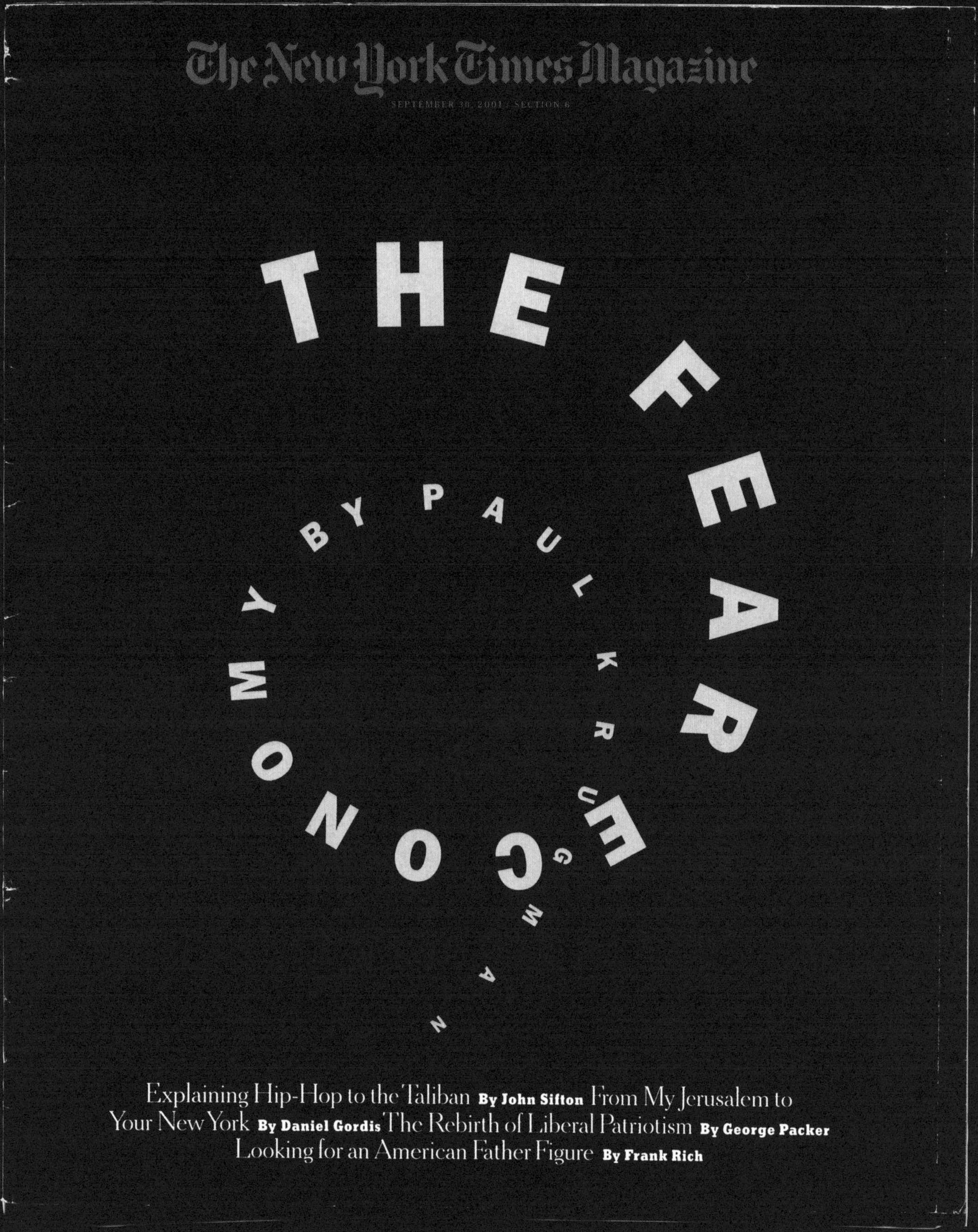

The New York Times Magazine

SEPTEMBER 30, 2001 / SECTION 6

THE FEAR ECONOMY

BY PAUL KRUGMAN

The New York Times Magazine

OCTOBER 29, 2006 / SECTION 6

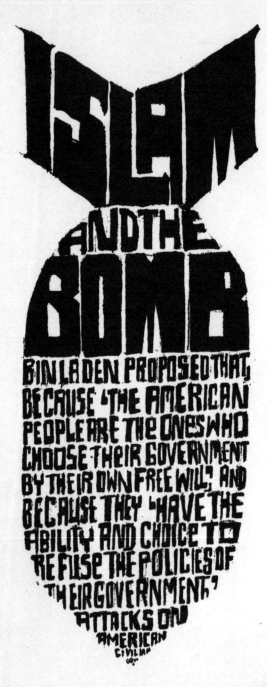

ISLAM AND THE BOMB

BIN LADEN PROPOSED THAT, BECAUSE 'THE AMERICAN PEOPLE ARE THE ONES WHO CHOOSE THEIR GOVERNMENT BY THEIR OWN FREE WILL', AND BECAUSE THEY 'HAVE THE ABILITY AND CHOICE TO REFUSE THE POLICIES OF THEIR GOVERNMENT', ATTACKS ON AMERICAN CIVILIANS

How to think — and not think — about the unspoken issue of the Second Nuclear Age.
By Noah Feldman

a Nuclear Iran will be a stronger and more effective enemy in pursuing anti-American policies under the banner of Islam

It will not change the Iranian state vendors either its Islamic identity

or its association between Islam and anti-Americanism

A Long Journey in the Dark

My life with chronic depression.
By Daphne Merkin

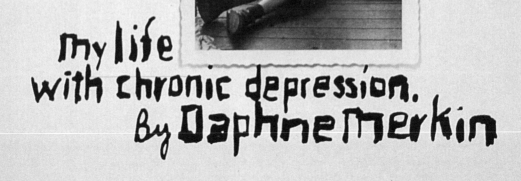

It is an affliction that often starts young and goes unheeded—younger than would seem possible, as if in exiting the womb I was enveloped in a gray and itchy wool blanket instead of a soft, pastel-colored bunting.

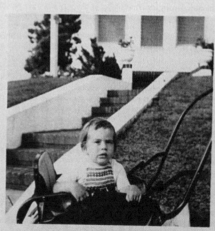

"Far better is it to dare mighty things, to win glorious triumphs, even though check-ered by failure . . . than to rank with those poor spirits who neither enjoy nor suffer much, because they live in a gray twi-light that knows not victory nor defeat."
—Theodore Roosevelt

20. End Discrimination

It was the perfect missed opportunity. I was contacted by the longtime creative director of Capitol Records, Tommy Steele, to create a full-spread advertisement for the record company's 2001 MTV Video Music Awards brochure. The theme of that year's awards show was simple enough: "end discrimination." All I had to do was to address this issue and use Capitol Records' classy little logo. I had the perfect client, the perfect format, and more importantly, the perfect audience: New York City's Metropolitan Op-era House, packed with hip, smart, and culturally savvy folks who would understand, enjoy, and embrace my message.

Clients hire me for a number of reasons, but being "safe" is not one of them. If I do not push my clients, then I am not doing my job. The idea of using the wrong-est imagery to belittle discrimination was funny to me at the time. Tommy Steele loved the idea, but admitted that it made him a bit nervous, too. He showed my image around Capitol's LA office and enjoyed the response from his coworkers. There seemed to be a delayed response of shock or disbelief, followed by "Aha! I get it!" Unfortunately, from there the sorry chain of command went like this: Tommy shows the work to the Capitol Records president, who does not understand the idea. Instead of trusting Steele—his creative director—he defers to his secre-tary, who disapproves. The job was killed. I have often threatened to print this image myself and distribute it freely. Maybe now I have.

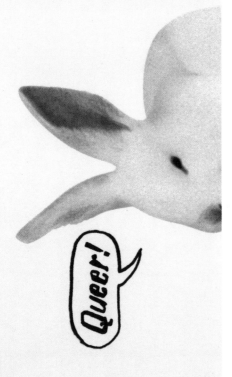

22.2

Disney Go Home
Just Say No

The idea to revitalize Times Square had been on the books since the early 1980s. In the late nineties, corporate donations helped make it happen, with Disney leading the way.

Disney? New York, I love you, but you're bringing me down. Becoming bland. Becoming a franchise. Selling yourself short in search of a buck, and the lowest form of a buck to boot—a tourist buck. We can now travel to any spot on the planet and find the exact same crap we have at home. Put a roof over it and call it a mall.

Feeling that I was again becoming Holden Caulfield–like (the only sane one, or, more likely, the only crazy one), I had to put in my two cents. I took a poster from a recent Syracuse University lecture (Figure 22.1) and reconstituted it, in two different versions. Disney Go Home was a take on the Vietnam-era slogan "Yankee go home"; Just Say No was a play on Nancy Reagan's famously lame stance on kids and drugs, which in turn was a take on Nike's much more effective slogan "Just do it." Both posters were designed in a "just get her done" style, silk-screened on whatever cheap paper my printer had available, and then hung throughout Times Square. In the corner, near the signature, it reads:

22.1

Images of an Ideal
Nation

The most memorable jobs are the ones with the best stories. DePaul University in Chicago held an exhibition of images from the labor, suffragette, civil rights, and antiwar movements by some of my heroes, including Alexander Calder and Ben Shahn, titled Images of an Ideal Nation. The idea of representing this "ideal" nation with a plucked American eagle seemed appropriate. American eagles being rather scarce, however, I opted instead for a Chinatown chicken, freshly killed and plucked. I dragged its still-warm carcass out onto my fire escape, where we styled it, photographed it, and then ate it.

OK, we didn't eat it, but it makes for a better story.

24.

Moët & Chandon

In Lao Tzu's *Tao Te Ching*, one encounters advice not only on governing oneself, but also on design. One such gem concerns simplicity and complexity. To wit, in simplicity there must be complexity, and in complexity there must be simplicity. This advice I've garnered from Henryk Tomaszewski, as well.

In complexity, today the trend is the glom—the end result of arranging similar visual items selected from stock, then adding a layer of words that all mean "good" set in various typefaces—a visual elbow in the ribs—to further drive one's point home. The point being not a point, but a gist. A whiff of an idea—just complexity alone. My career has been spent as a whittler, one who, in an effort to find the kernel of truth buried within an idea, cuts away all excess, thus arriving at a point.

This, of course, has nothing to do with the fact that champagne and sex go well together—non?

23.

Choose or Lose

We lost.

23.1

E PLURIBUS UNUM

IMAGES of an IDEAL NATION

Images Of An Ideal Nation

An Exhibition of Images from the American Social and Political
Movements of the Nineteenth and Twentieth Centuries

DePaul University Art Gallery
April 9 to May 16, 1998

22.1

dr LOSE 200t

CHOOSE

MTV
MUSIC TELEVISION©

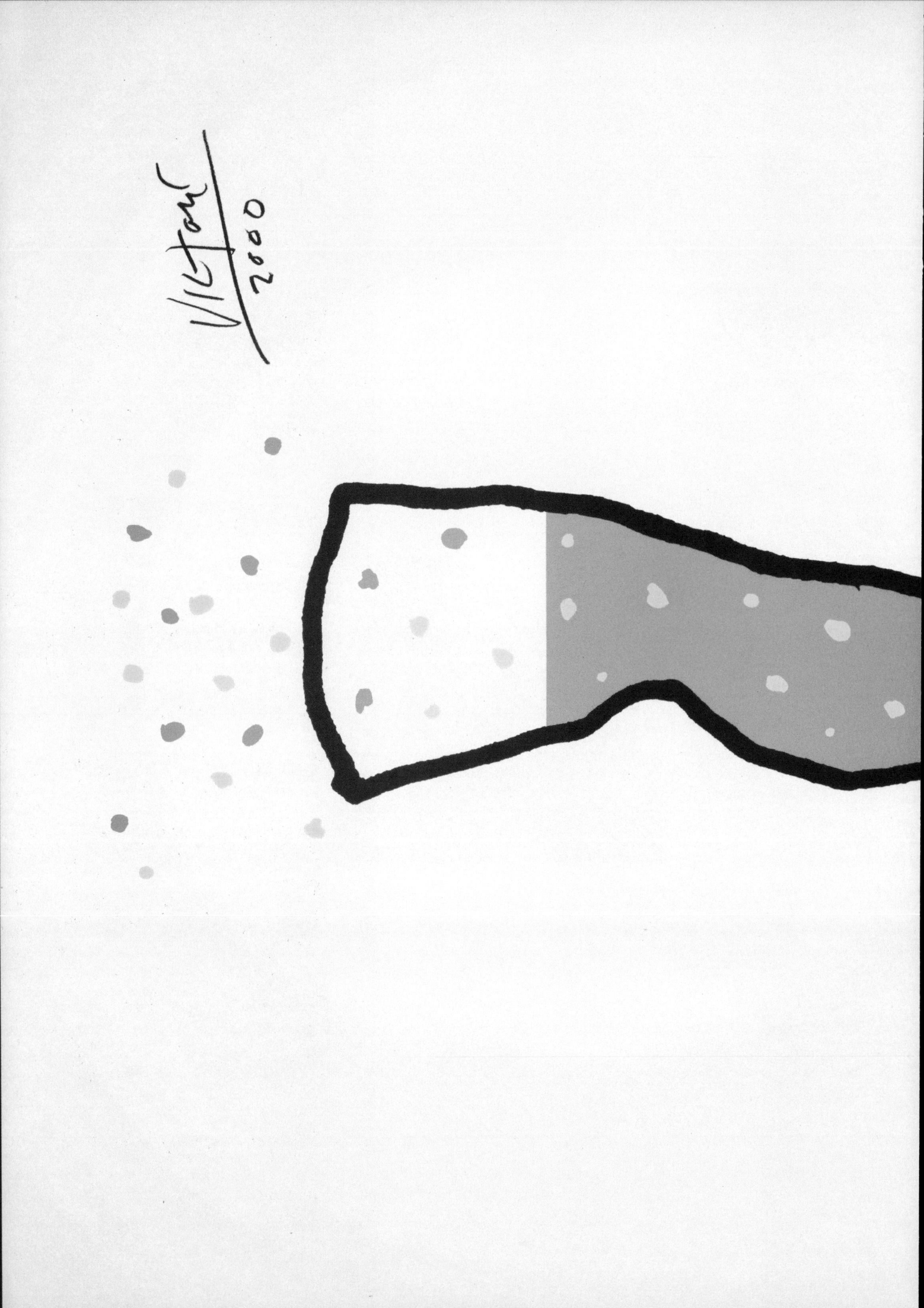

MOËT & CHANDON

PAR JAMES VICTORE

25. Come

The 2001 AIGA (the professional association for design) "Voice" design conference was to be held in Washington, DC, in late September. I was invited to design a postcard to announce the event. At the time, the country was still reeling from George Bush's stolen election. For designers, this was an opportunity to go, en masse, marching to the United States Capitol to express our opinions and show our strength and unity. To gain the attention we both deserved and craved.

I personally felt so strongly about this opportunity that within this group of conference attendees zooming into the Capitol I hid a Russian MiG jet, a symbol of the power our "voice" could have.

Twelve days before the conference was to be held, four commercial airliners were taken by hijackers; one was slammed into the Pentagon in Arlington, Virginia, one into a field in Pennsylvania, and two into Towers 1 and 2 of the World Trade Center in New York City.

25.1

25.2

26.ab

2 M

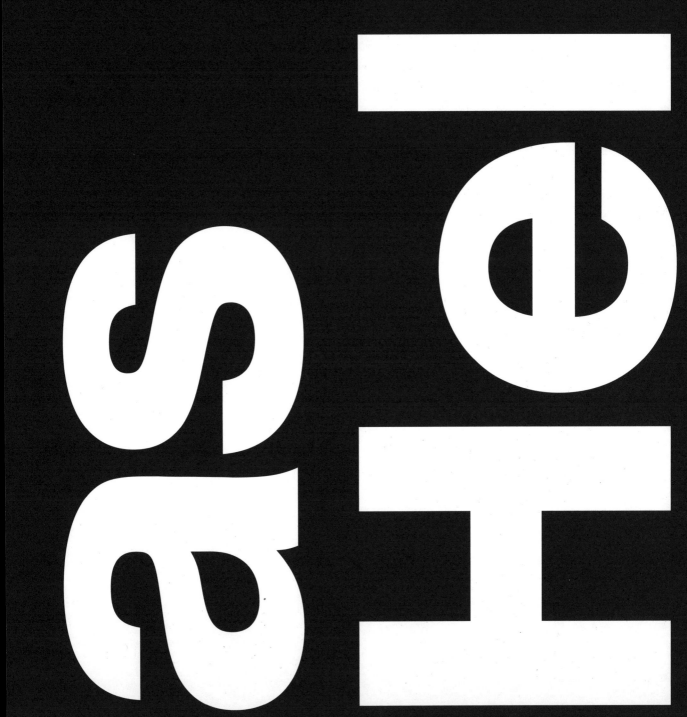

AIGA NEW YORK presents

JAMES VICTORE

Wednesday, October 16, 2002
Haft Auditorium, FIT
in Lovely New York City

HELL

photography: Thomas Schierlitz

I was reared on a military base during the Vietnam War. From this I learned two important things: (1) good posture and (2) to question authority. In my room hung a very intricate psychedelic poster of . . . I don't know what, and an antiwar poster that read:

TRAVEL TO EXOTIC PLACES,
MEET INTERESTING PEOPLE,
AND KILL THEM.

VIET NAM.

(This poster taught me irony.) Having a military background produced deep emotions in me. I love my country and therefore feel comfortable asking difficult questions of it.

"Mad as Hell" was my homecoming, my first lecture in post–9/11 New York City. Sponsored by AIGA, it was held on a cold and rainy October eve, during a bad economy, but people came, and it was a party. We made posters to sell (Bush Pirate) and created a short music video (Bush Flag over Iraq, Figure 26.2), and a six-foot-tall gorilla in pink high heels delivered me a beer onstage.

During the post-lecture Q and A, someone asked why I was "mad as hell," my response was, "Because nobody else is." Originally, the subtitle for the lecture was "Patriot, Citizen, Father, Commie-Pinko-Fag." The fact that the paper company that sponsored the event made me censor the subtitle on the poster only proved my point.

As for the title here, it is a not-very-subtle reference to Peter Finch's famous line from the 1976 film *Network*: "I'm mad as hell, and I'm not gonna take it anymore." But the truth is, we do take it. Again and again. I am not sure why there is so little dissent these days. Maybe most people are like me, trying to make rent, taking on too many jobs just to stay afloat. Or maybe we are too distracted by our iPhones, TiVos, video games, or Facebook to really pay attention. Maybe we're asleep at the wheel.

"Habits are human nature— why not create some that will mint Gold?"
—Hafiz, *The Subject Tonight Is Love*

26.2

27. Nouveau Salon des Cent

Une exposition organisée par le designer Néerlandais Anthon Beeke. Anthon a invité ceux lequel il s'est senti étaient les grands petits-enfants de Toulouse-Lautrec.

Exposition Internationale d'affiches
Hommage à Toulouse-Lautrec

MICHEL BATORY

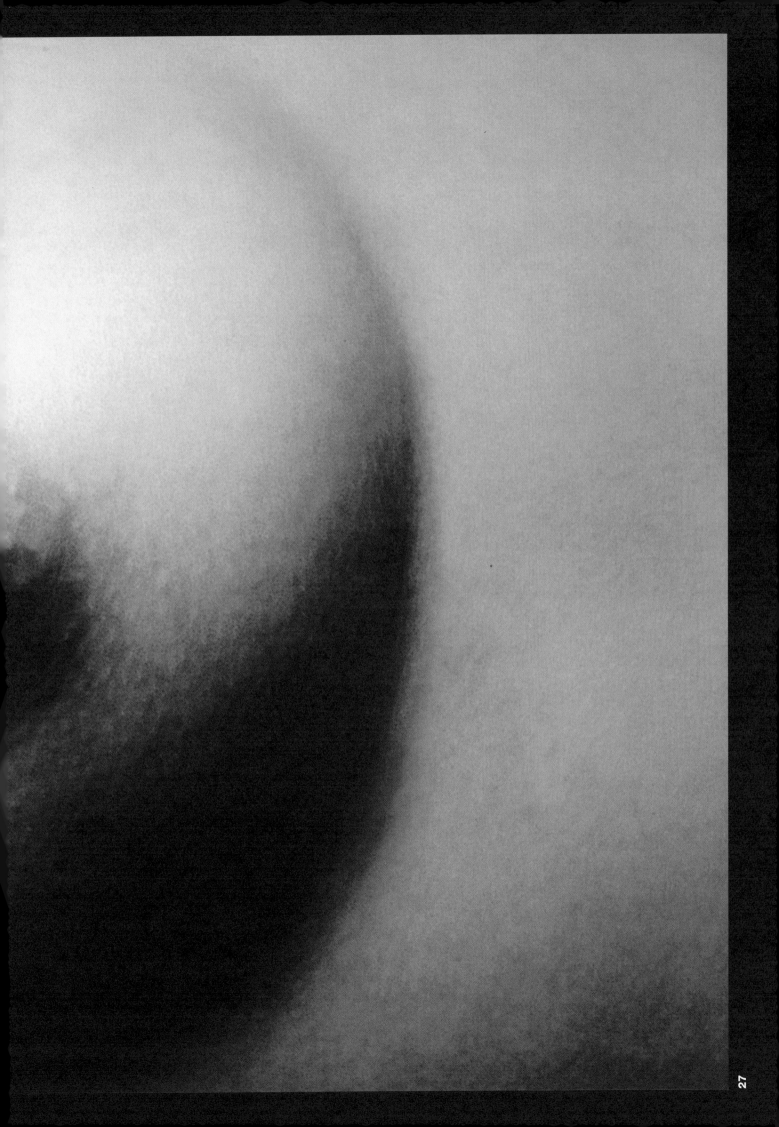

28. Bush Pirate

After 9/11, the U.S. military response was to extract revenge. George Bush was in charge and was raping and pillaging at will. Less than a month after the attacks here, the United States mounted an air and ground attack against Afghanistan, a shadowy offensive in search of al Qaeda mastermind Osama bin Laden, as well as nuclear, chemical, and biological weapons, none of which were ever found. By January 2002 Bush labeled Iran, Iraq, and North Korea the "Axis of Evil." Americans prepared for the "war for re- sources," and rushed out to buy flags and yellow ribbons for their cars.

This poster was originally created as a fund-raiser for an AIGA event. Publishing and distributing an anti-Bush poster in New York City, where practically everyone already agrees with you, seemed to me a silly en- deavor. With a minimum of research, I made contact with an organization called International A.N.S.W.E.R. (Act Now to Stop War and End Racism), which was organizing large-scale pre–Iraq War marches in Washington, DC, New York, and San Francisco. I collected all the unsold AIGA posters and paid to print additional copies, then donated the lot to A.N.S.W.E.R. I wanted to cover the marches with these flags and turn them into an army, a movement.

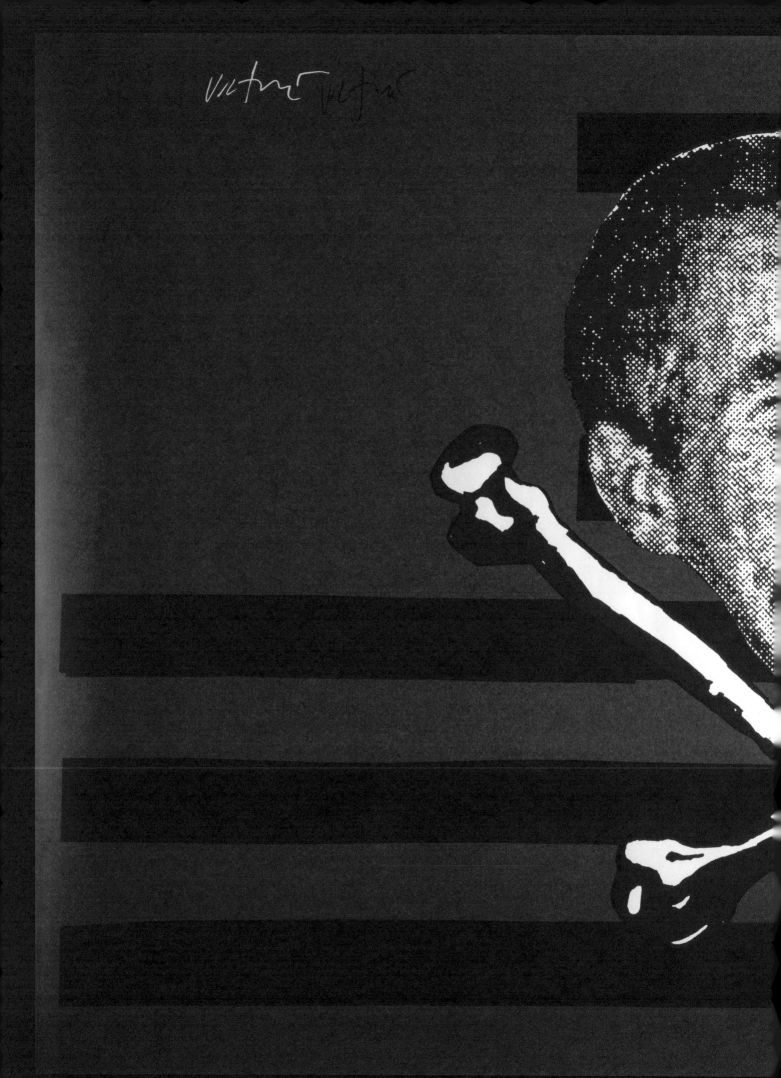

29.
SVA

Barely halfway through the School of Visual Arts, I was taken aside by one of my instructors and told that I should consider becoming a CPA or maybe a ski instructor. I took his advice and dropped out. I was uninspired, bored, and boring. Higher education was just not in the cards for me.

Not exactly the beginning of a love story—but for the last fifteen years I have been teaching at the School of Visual Arts. My long relationship with the school is one of

29.1

which I am most proud.

Silas Rhodes, the founder of SVA, was the type of creative director I moved to New York to find. More of a patron of the arts than a client, he was a creative visionary who hired talent and let them create with little interference (or at least that was true in my case). Silas gave me the opportunity to work on one of the greatest assignments in the world: New York City Subway posters for the school. I had no other mandate than to attract attention to and advertise SVA. I turned this into an opportunity to express everything I loved about New York (Beach Family, Figure 29.2) and to teach Rilke in the subway (Live the Questions, Figure 29.4).

When the press proof for the Rilke poster arrived in the studio, we hung it up on the wall for judgment. Immediately those in the studio were struck by one thing: the size of my signature. It seems that I had finally grown too big for my britches, or my ego. But I have always signed my work. This seemed normal to me. I've always wanted to take responsibility for the words and ideas, but more importantly, I've always wanted the viewer-receiver to know that a human being made the work and that they, too, in their own way, could make the work.

ART IN SERVICE TO INDUSTRY

The designer is not always right. The researcher is not always wrong. Profit is not always the motive; market research, whatever its outcome, should never be used as a good excuse for bad design—in the same sense that good design should never be used to promote a bad product.—Paul Rand

~ j'allais sous le ciel,
Muse! et j'étais
ton féal ~
—rimbaud

The designer is not always right. The researcher is not always wrong. Profit is not always the motive; market research, whatever its outcome, should never be used as a good excuse for bad design—in the same sense that good design should never be used to promote a bad product.—Paul Rand

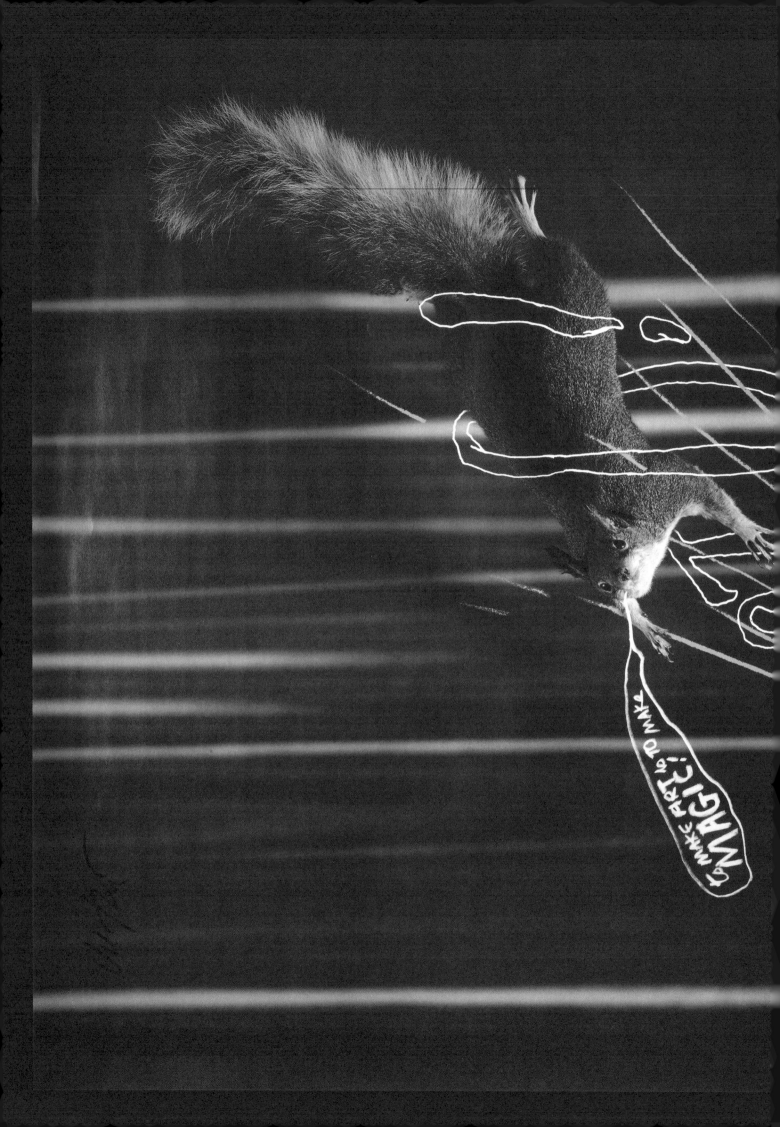

MAGIC! to make ART to make

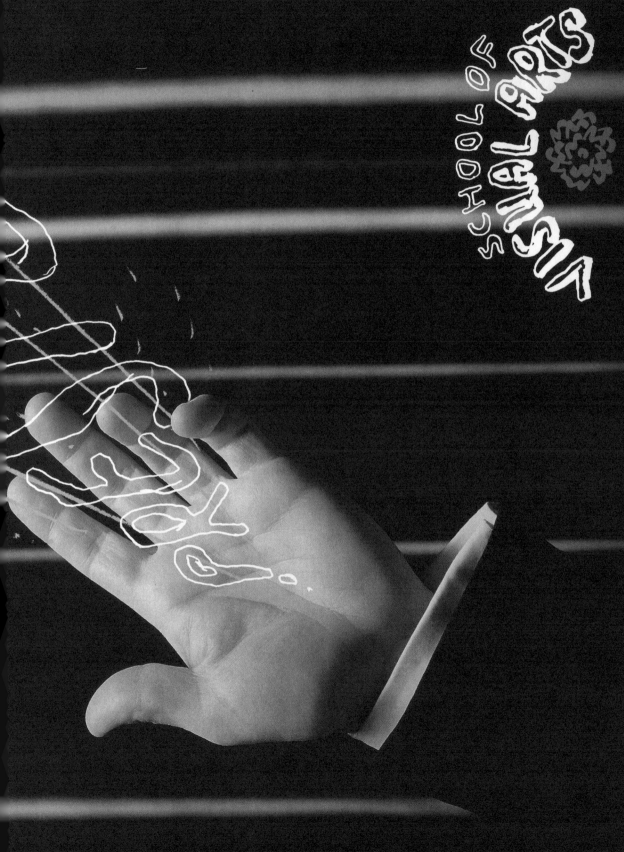

SCHOOL OF VISUAL ARTS

UNDERGRADUATE PROGRAMS Advertising | Animation | Art History | Cartooning | Computer Art | Film & Video | Fine Arts
Graphic Design | Humanities & Sciences | Illustration | Interior Design | Photography GRADUATE PROGRAMS Art
Criticism | Art Education | Art Therapy | Computer Art | Design | Fine Arts | Illustration as Visual Essay | Photography,
Video and Related Media CONTINUING EDUCATION DIVISION School of VISUAL ARTS
209 East 23rd Street, Beautiful New York City, 10010-3994 Tel: 800.366.7820 Fax: 212.725.3587 www.schoolofvisualarts.edu
Creative Director: Silas Rhodes Art Director / Designer: James Victore Photographer: Jean Schwartz Writer: Dee Ito
Copyright ©2003 by School of Visual Arts Press

LIVE the QUES

(DON'T SEARCH for ANSWERS, whi[ch] [could]
not be given to you now, because you w[ould not be able]
to live them. And the point is to live ev[erything])

Perhaps then, someday far in the future, you will gradually, without even noticing it, live your way into the answer.
—R.M. Rilke
LETTERS to a YOUNG POET

...could not be able ...thing.

Ludvasher @

School of VISUAL ARTS

209 East 23 Street, Beautiful New York City, 10010-3994 Tel: 212.592.2000 Fax: 212.725.3587 www.sva.edu
Creative Director: Silas Rhodes | Designer: James Victore
Copyright © 2007, Visual Arts Press, LTD.
From Letters to a Young Poet by Rainer Maria Rilke, Courtesy of Stephen Mitchell (translator), Dover Publications.

This file folder is intended to help Urgent Action activists keep all the paperwork associated with the program together and organized. It is suggested that the Urgent Actions, follow-ups and the monthly UA Newsletter, be kept in the right side while the letter-writing guide and other program-related papers stay on the left.

Additional folders are available at no cost upon request. The UA Network includes activists of all ages working individually and in schools, local Amnesty International Chapters and, through the Inter-religious UA Network, at religious services.

My class of 5th and 6th graders write many letters in response to your Children's Edition UA Appeals. It is something they can do in a world where they often feel helpless.
—Ann Angell, Atlanta, Georgia

I still sense that this is one of the most important efforts I could possibly make and that is a lot at age 78!
—Donald Littlejohn, Eureka, Illinois

Thank you for the opportunity to be useful to persons in need.
—Rabbi Max Selinger, Kinson, North Carolina

30. Urgent Action

The Urgent Action Network is an adjunct office of Amnesty International. It was founded in 1975 by Ellen Moore and Scott Harrison and, until 2006, was directed by them from their home office in northern Colorado. News of human rights abuses are transmitted from AI to the UAN, which mobilizes individuals, schools, religious groups, and professional and special interest groups worldwide to contact those in power, demanding that the violations be stopped. The accused authorities, deluged by mail, quickly realize that their actions are witnessed by an international audience. The UAN literally saves lives every day.

I sought out the UAN after I received a fifty-thousand-dollar grant from the paper company Sappi to work with a nonprofit organization to enhance

their communications. At the time, the UAN had no communication materials to speak of, just over-Xeroxed newspaper clippings stuffed into manila folders and mailed to prospective constituents.

I generally despise "branding." It should be limited to what farmers do to cattle and sheep, not a business designers get involved in. But it is sometimes a necessary evil, and, like any design practice, can be used for good. For UAN, the thin veneer of graphic design I added—color and a few fonts—lent the organization the validity and professionalism they lacked. But branding can all too easily go the way of the dark side. This now-specialized form of design studies human beings and their habits and actions, then targets them as a market, just to shovel more crap onto their bathroom shelves and into their kitchen closets and storage facilities, in an attempt to give the people "what they want." As a culture we are over-branded, oversimplified, and overfed—but still undernourished. I fear the day some idiot figures out how to brand air and sell it back to us.

URGENT ACTION

Save Lives. Stop Torture. Secure Human Rights. Join the Urgent Action Network. This volunteer network mobilizes for men, women, and children worldwide who are facing torture, "disappearance", execution, or other life-threatening violations of their basic human rights. Amnesty International compiles information every day, year round, on people who urgently need public action. *Your action.*

Amnesty International will provide you with a description of the prisoner's situation, names and addresses of authorities in positions to protect the person at risk, and guidelines for writing appeals to those authorities.

Mail. Fax. Email. Web. You choose how you want to receive Urgent Action cases. You choose how to send your appeals.

AMNESTY INTERNATIONAL is a worldwide grassroots movement that promotes and defends human rights. It works independently of all governments and political ideologies to secure the release of prisoners of conscience, ensure fair and prompt trials for political prisoners, and end torture, political killings, "disappearances," and the death penalty.

The Urgent Action Network is one of Amnesty International's most effective volunteer groups. Initiated in 1973 and continuously incorporating the most rapid communications technologies available, the Network operates 24 hours a day, 7 days a week, every day of the year.

TAKE URGENT ACTION

SAVE LIVES. STOP TORTURE. SECURE HUMAN RIGHTS

www.amnestyusa.org/urgent/
1.800.AMNESTY, ext. UAN

"Art is not truth, art is a lie that makes us realize the truth."
—Picasso

31. Medea

"Hell hath no fury like a woman scorned." —William Congreve

32. Aveda

Every year, the forward-thinking cosmetic company Aveda runs a campaign to raise both awareness and money for nonprofit conservation organizations. It is a rare privilege to work with crazy people with money who are interested in doing good work and giving back.

Not all commercial poster/campaign jobs turn out this good. Some jobs you do for God and some you do for money. Rarely, as was the case in this instance, is it both. I start all jobs as "God jobs," an opportunity to create great work. But, occasionally, if fate turns it into a money job, I swallow my pride, give the client what they want, and get paid.

My choice to maintain a small studio stems from this conundrum. If, as a designer, I seek approval in the form of fees for my work, and base my output solely on those fees being paid, I risk the possibility of doing bad work. Staying small, having only one or two assistants, and keeping a low overhead helps me maintain flexibility and a level of commitment to the work, and gives me the choice of just how much shit I have to eat.

"'But you were always a good man of business, Jacob,' faltered Scrooge, who now began to apply this to himself. 'Business!' cried the Ghost, wringing its hands again. 'Mankind was my business. The common welfare was my business; charity, mercy, forbearance, and benevolence, were, all, my business. The dealings of my trade were but a drop of water in the comprehensive ocean of my business!'" —Charles Dickens, *A Christmas Carol*

33. Hero/ Victim

In 2003 I was invited to contribute my work to an exhibition in the Netherlands. The show, titled Armour: The Fortification of Man, was organized around the idea that we defend our inner selves with art, architecture, design, and fashion. In lieu of sending existing work, I designed a set of buttons—the kind that are handed out at museums after you pay the entrance fee. The buttons were distributed randomly; you were not allowed to choose which one (Hero or Victim) you received. This small act of creative terrorism forced visitors to face themselves, to take a position.

Many visitors were unnerved by this, and some looked to trade their button. At the opening, the curator of the exhibition, Li Edelkoort, made a short film from interviewing attendees, asking each person, "Are you a hero or a victim?" Curiously, most attendees felt more comfortable with the label of "victim" than that of "hero."

34. Chronogram

Chronogram is a health and New Age magazine published in upstate New York. This cover had nothing to do with the magazine's content; I simply love this Cherokee story. After the magazine came out, I received so many requests for the "poster" version of the cover that I wish I had made one.

35. GQ/Aristocrats

Stand-up comedians have an inside joke with the punch line " ...the Aristocrats!" The joke itself is not important, and maybe it isn't even funny. The important thing is how well the content is improvised. In 2005, comedians Penn Jillette and Paul Provenza turned this dirty joke into a full-length film that featured their favorite comedians retelling the joke. The Aristocrats is riotously funny—and completely disgusting. I was asked by GQ magazine to create a page devoted to the film. The image reproduced as Figure 35 is what I sent and what was accepted and paid for. When the magazine hit newsstands I searched for the fanny, but the fanny was missing. I called the creative director and was told that at the last minute, the editors decided the image was "too sexy" for GQ. Too sexy for GQ? Are you fucking kidding me?

the Ticket you Couldn't get

/UNTIL NOW

"In this thrilling production, Greek TRAGEDY'S MOST SPECTACULARLY VENGEFUL WOMAN has REMATERIALIZED as the MOST ESSENTIAL TICKET of this THEATER SEASON. The show RADIATES SUCH HIGH THEATRICAL ENERGY and INSIGHT THAT YOU CAN'T HELP GRINNING THROUGH MOST of it. Fiona SHAW and DEBORAH WARNER have CREATED one of the MOST HUMAN MEDEAS EVER."

— (I)SLEY, THE NEW YORK TIMES
10.4.02

"This MEDEA comes at us WITH the SLEEK SWIFTNESS of a BULLET TRAIN. IT IS THE KIND of ENRICHING and TERRIFYING NIGHT in the THEATER THAT NOT ONLY CAN MAKE FOR AN INVIGORATING RIDE home, BUT ALSO, IN THE HOURS to FOLLOW, A FITFUL SLEEP. AVERT YOUR EYES? NOT A CHANCE."

— PETER MARKS, THE WASHINGTON POST
11.8.02

Directed by Deborah WARNER

→ 84 PERFORMANCES ONLY
Begins December 4

Call today TICKETMASTER.COM 212-307-4100/800-755-4000

Groups: 212-398-8383/800-223-7565

BROOKS ATKINSON THEATRE, 256 West 47th STREET

save plants
save yourself

AVEDA
the art and science of pure flower and plant essences

32.1

32.2

33

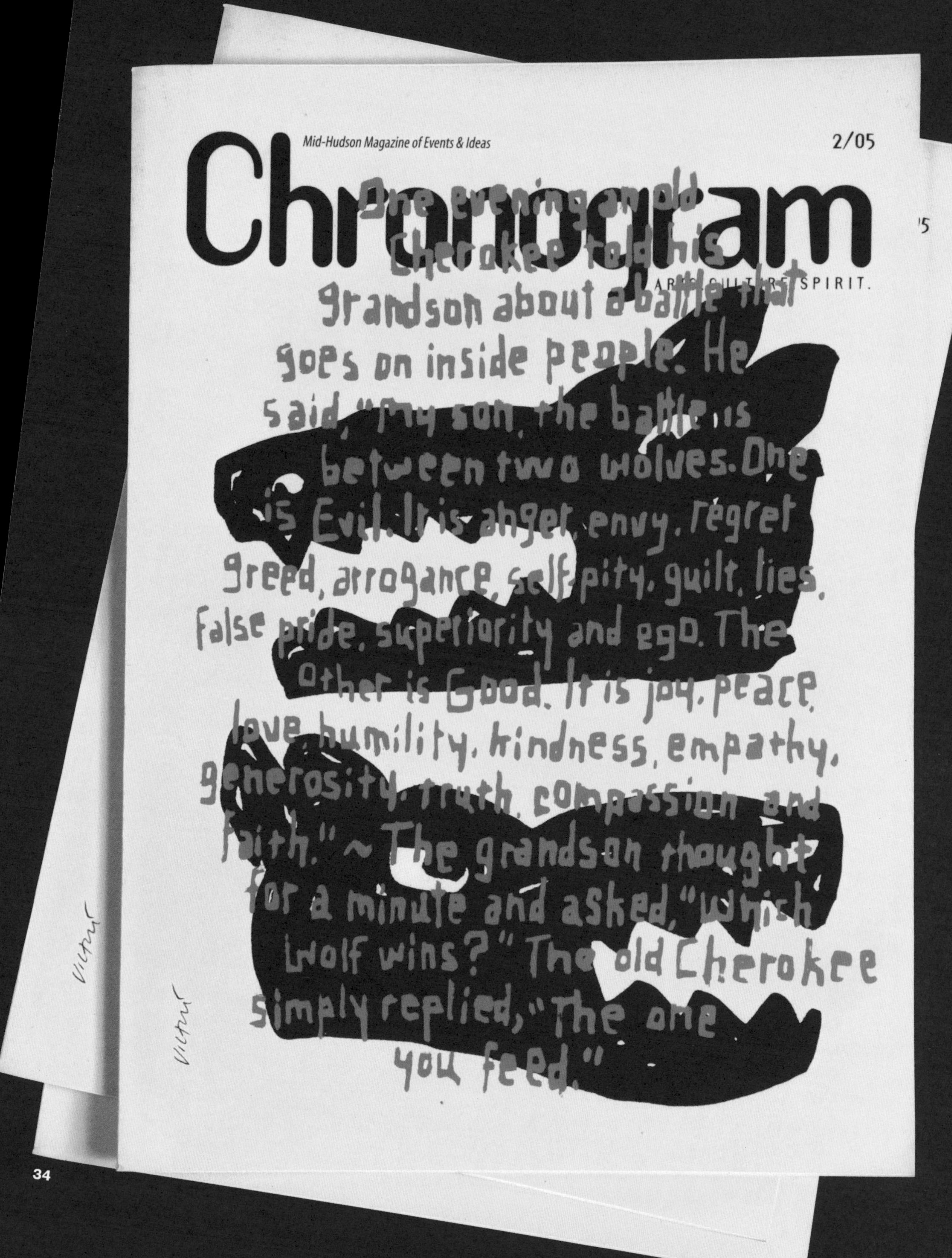

Chronogram

ART. CULTURE. SPIRIT.

One evening an old Cherokee told his grandson about a battle that goes on inside people. He said, "My son, the battle is between two wolves. One is Evil. It is anger, envy, regret greed, arrogance, self-pity, guilt, lies, false pride, superiority and ego. The Other is Good. It is joy, peace, love, humility, kindness, empathy, generosity, truth, compassion and faith." ~ The grandson thought for a minute and asked, "which wolf wins?" The old Cherokee simply replied, "The one you feed."

Victor

Victor

Victor

34

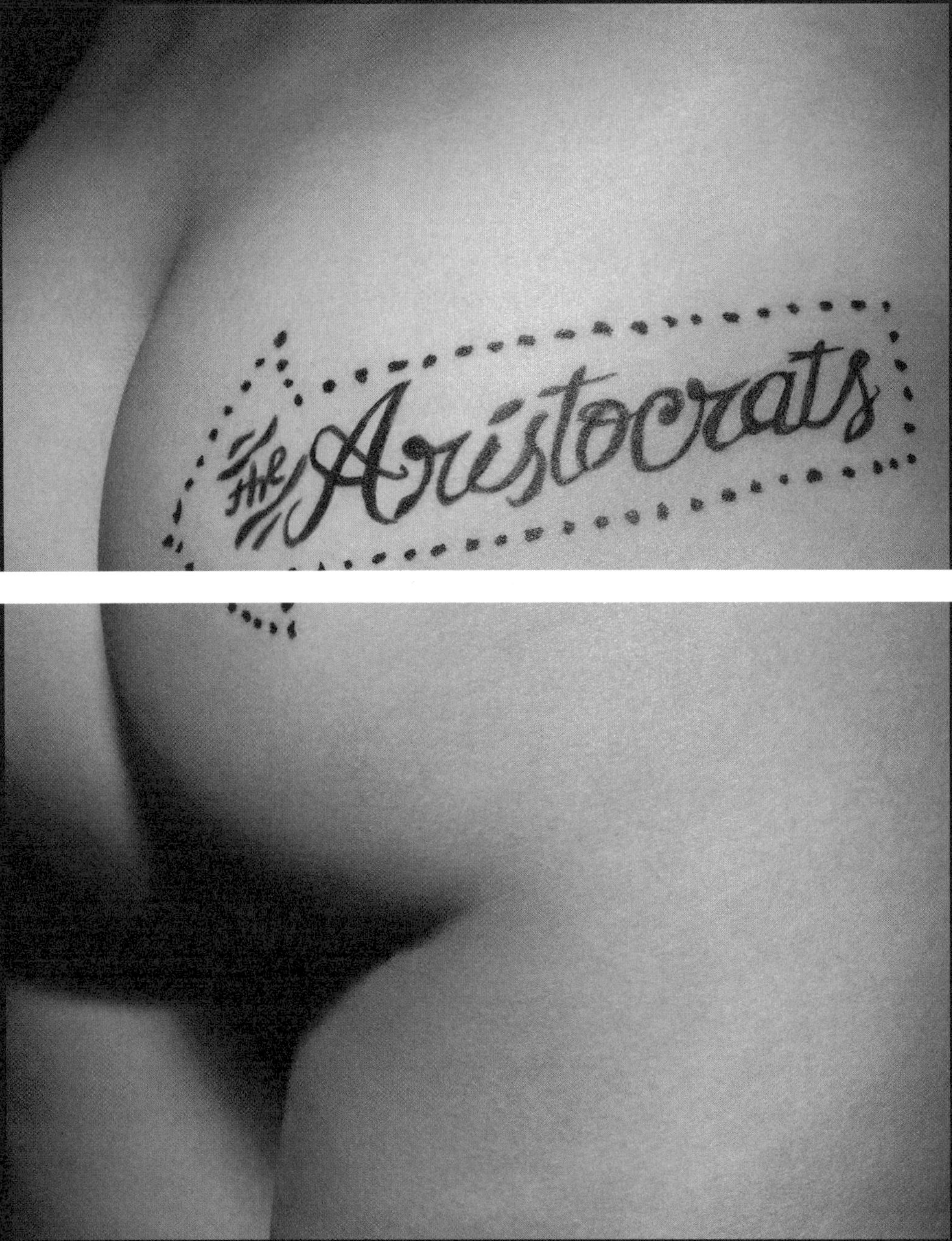
The Aristocrats

INSTIGATOR
presents

James Victore's Dirty Dishes

SEPTEMBER 11 through OCTOBER 30 2005
OPENING RECEPTION SEPT 11 at 5 pm.
INSTIGATOR 220 NORTH 8TH STREET
WILLIAMSBURG, BROOKLYN NYC 11211
718·388·2426

36. Plates

My best work is for an audience of one. A get-well card for a family member; a surprise note to my son in his lunch box; or a small, collaged, painted smeared postcard for a friend. These projects have a spirit and warmth that I try to bring to my daily work.

When I was a young designer, my apartment was never much to speak of, and my "studio" nonexistent. I often sought out a satellite studio in a local bar, pub, or restaurant. This was not the ideal setup but always yielded interesting results. My habit of drawing on everything is enhanced after a drink or two, and facilitated by the Sharpie marker I always carry with me. Inhibitions gone, I would invariably end up drawing on the establishment's plates, sometimes trading bread-plate drawings for a beer or a cute bartender's phone number. Over the years I have made hundreds of one-of-a-kind plates, most of them mementos for friends.

In 2005, my pal the designer and curator Paul Weston invited me to have a show of my poster work in his four-hundred-square-foot gallery, aptly named Instigator. I told him I would think about it, but I didn't have much interest in showing posters. The next month, on a trip to Austin, I stopped

to visit my friend and fellow designer Christian Helms. We were casually chatting in his studio when I noticed a delightful little drawing of a skull and crossbones, on a blue-rimmed butter plate. I immediately became jealous, until I realized that I had drawn the plate for Christian when he was in New York earlier that year. Eureka! We called the show Dirty Dishes.

We become what we pretend to be, and I had become the plate guy. As the Dishes show neared the end of its month-long run, I received a call from Ray Brunner, CEO of the retail chain Design Within Reach. Ray was a friend of mine and was on my invitation list for the Dirty Dishes show. He thought the show sounded "like a good idea" and wanted to put the plates up at DWR. As soon as the show came down at Instigator, it moved to DWR's studio/store in New York's Meatpacking District. In order to have a strong presence in DWR's three-thousand-square-foot space, I painted a hundred additional plates.

Lately, to gain more control of this medium, I have begun experimenting with ceramics, creating plates from raw clay. Initially I became a designer because I liked working with my hands, and now I am back at it. In design school today there is much less emphasis on drawing and making. We are completely competent at teaching computer skills, but forget step number one—the ability to draw and create with your hands is imperative to understanding design and form. I never want to lose the joy of making something for the pure sake of making it.

I ♥
N
MORE
MIL
GLF

Y
THAN
ON
SER

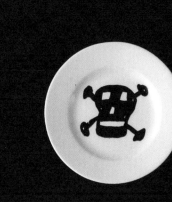

luc

EAT
BUSH

36.3

Laura

BLACKPOOL

fresh culture magazine
novembre/décembre/janvier

37. Blackpool

I have always held the belief that I, and designers in general, hail from a long line of artists, misfits, and anarchists. My heroes have always been cowboys—people who have something to say and put it into their work. Artists like John Heartfield, Ben Shahn, Picasso, Warhol, the Dadaists, the Atelier Populaire, Johnny Cash, Bob Marley, and Bob Dylan.

Blackpool is a French cultural magazine. The cover, an homage to Marcel Duchamp. And chance. And boobies.

38. Yohji

The phone rings. Sometimes it is the wolf, tired of knocking. Sometimes it is a client, come from the left-est part of left field, out of the blue, even, whom I, in a million years, could never have guessed would ring me up. I am not known for my work in the fashion industry, so the call I got one day from the Japanese fashion maestro Yohji Yamamoto was completely unexpected.

The French designer Pierre Bernard has been quoted as saying, "In order for creative work to take place we must have a creative designer, a creative client, a creative printer and a creative audience." With Yohji, I had all of these—

and I never felt more inadequate. Yohji himself is one of the most talented designers of any type working today. He inspires with his work, hires talent, and lets them do their damn job.

Then he urges them to do more.

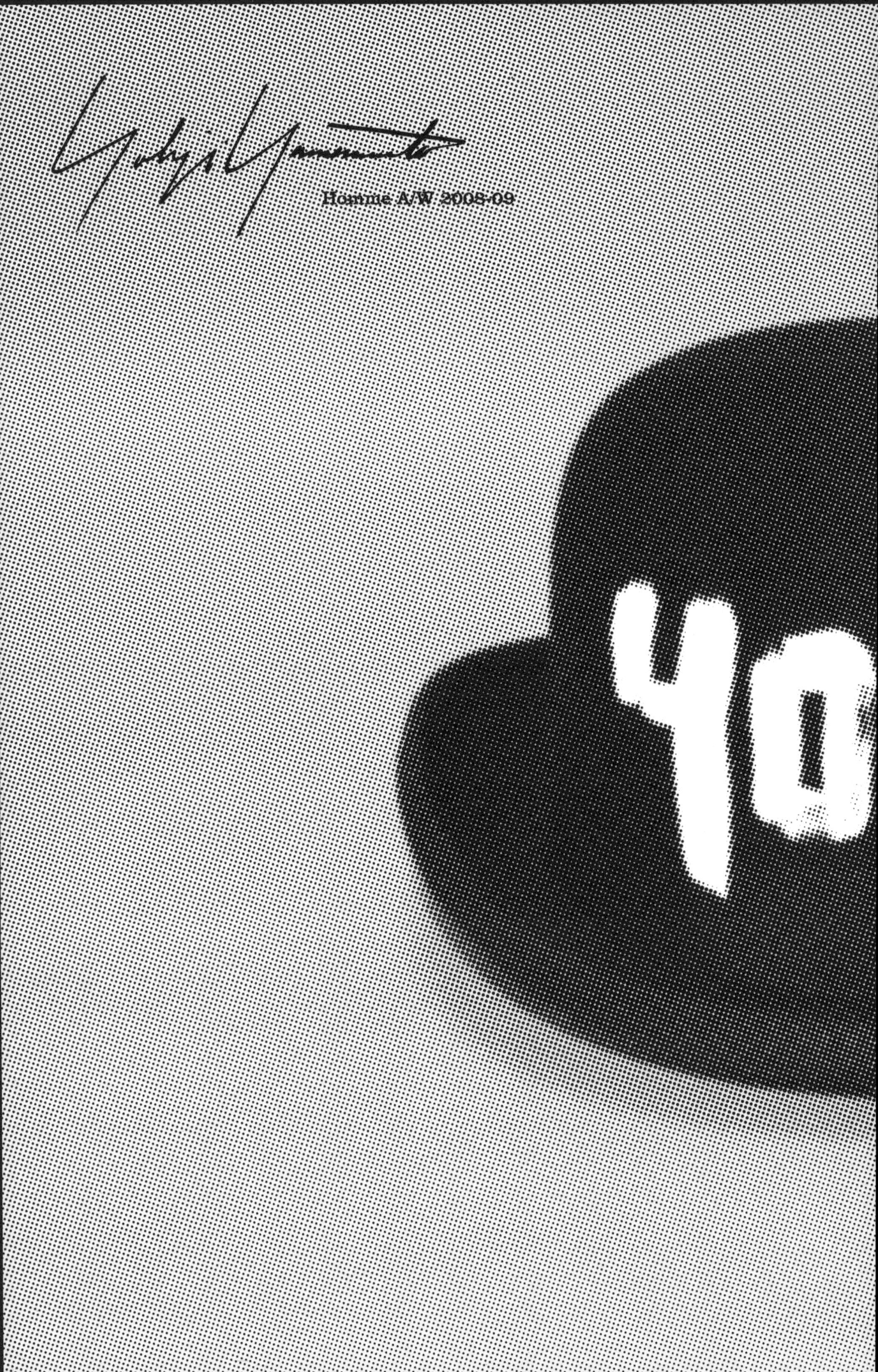
Homme A/W 2008-09

09
s/s

Yohji Yamamoto

38.3

39. Surfboards

I am a born customizer. I draw on everything, including myself; my arms are prominently tatooed with the names "Luca" and "Laura." As a kid I was fascinated by the customized world of Kar Kulture, steeped in Ed "Big Daddy" Roth and his hot-rod character Rat Fink, and Revell models (with that wonderful glue). But really, Hot Wheels die-cast toy cars were my biggest influence. My favorite of these scale-model hot rods were the most chopped, bobbed, shaved, lowered, painted-up prima donna cars available. Hell, I even repainted my favorites until they lost all of their tiny little model details. Not bad for a kid reared in the northeast corner of New York State, thousands of miles from the car shows of Pomona.

In search of a new longboard for myself, I found a board shaper, Mike Becker, who was game to work with me. My designer pal and fellow surfer Paul Sahre and I came home from Mike's Long Island shop with nine blank boards in the back of my pickup. Our intent was to customize them. Not to sell them or exhibit them or even to ride them. We just wanted to play. To paint, draw, and customize.

Again, Ray Brunner, hearing of the excitement I was trying to make, invited me to create a limited-edition board for Design Within Reach. I have not dropped the design game for the custom surfboard game. The worldwide clientele for hand-painted boards numbers around ten, and I have already sold to seven of them.

39.1

James Victore Surfboard (2007)

DESIGNER: James Victore

US Blanks-made polyurethane foam; Hexcel® fiberglass.

H 74" W 18.25" 13464 **$3000**

"What dangerous curves and me with no brakes," are the Spanish words you'll be reading (or screaming) as you carve your way down a breaking wave. And James Victore's hand-painted artwork isn't the only thing that's bold about this board. Designed for the hurricane-loving dawn patroller, this 6'2" shortboard is hand-shaped and glassed by Mike Becker of Nature's Shapes in Long Island, and outfitted with three Future fins. Victore is a self-taught artist and designer known for his emotive, sensual and fearless work. His clients include the *New York Times*, Apple and Yamaha. He is also a professor at the School of Visual Arts in New York.

Teaching

—and jobs don't love you.

If you do something long enough you will eventually get good at it, or become bored—disillusioned—and move on to some other endeavor. I have been teaching steadily for fifteen years at SVA, as well as lecturing and conducting workshops worldwide, and have just now maybe hit my stride. The most recent venue is with co-conspirators Paul Sahre and Jan Wilker, in our creatively titled summer workshop "Sahre Victore Wilker."

One would think that having no design education to speak of, having never learned the proper way to do, well, anything, would tend to be a major handicap. Instead, it allows me to for-go the formalities and head right into the good stuff.

Early in my teaching career I thought there was some lesson or a few rules I was supposed to impart to my charges. It took some time listening to the students, really seeing what was going on in the classroom before I realized what the students wanted, what they needed, and what they came to me for. And any rules I could donate to their cause would fit in a shoe box and would only qualify them to get a job

Most students enter class with a prognostication of what their future in the design business holds. And generally it is not a pretty picture. When it is suggested that they widen their perspective or entertain a radical idea, or just shoot for the moon, I am met with that lamentable moan, "But, Mr. Victore . . . In the real world . . . ." These students are not even out the door, haven't yet had their first whiff of rejection, and are already braced for it. This, of course, is natural, as they have already been trained in design. Trained by twenty years of sitting in front of the TV. Of looking at the colorful—but "new" and inevitably "improved"—sadness that fills the supermarket. Of watching movies marketed to them, made from a formula, and the only memorable bit was a fart joke. They are unwittingly trained in corporate- and committee-approved design. They have been trained to "obey."

Students want the truth. I completely understand this desire. We've been raised on Cheez Whiz and Count Chocula, standardized testing and fake boobs, fake wrestling and fake presidents. I've only got one truth. Fart jokes are funny—but only for a little while—and love always wins. If we can, through our work, cut through the clutter and make some statement another human being can recognize and about which they can say, "Yes, this is how it's supposed to be—this is how we really are," then all the fart jokes in the world, are, well, just fart jokes.

My job is to foster that desire for the truth. To stoke that fire. We all have different backgrounds, and each a different purpose, but we all have one commonality—a story to tell. It is my job to help students find their voice. Like any good shrink, I have to figure out the right questions to ask so that they can access that story and put it into the work. Too many times during critiques I see a disconnect, an alignment problem between what the student says and the crap they put on the wall. I try to have them understand the value of their story, of their opinion, and put that in the work. I want them to understand the potential they have as designers to bring about real change—and not just decorate someone else's package. To remind them that hard work matters, and there are no shortcuts. It is my job to awaken these possibilities in my students.

Students want answers, but graphic design is not math.

The only answers are the ones we are born with, and we must become comfortable with that. We have to become comfortable, and comfortable being uncomfortable. And ultimately, it's the questions that are more interesting anyway. I want to turn all my students into five-year-olds, and make them ask "Why?" all the time. To ask it about their work, and their lives, and the world around them. Because deep inside all the "whys" they might find out who they really are and where all their ideas come from. I push them to be brave, to kill the tiny critic inside them and trust their ideas and themselves. I often sound like Barney (yes, the purple dinosaur), pleading to students, "Just be yourself."

I want to let students and young professionals know that they matter and their opinions matter. In the commercial world, we fight for this. In teaching, we have to foster it. I want more misfits. I want to create strong, funny, spiked-club-wielding giants who leave a mark wherever they go. I want to teach them to go find good clients. And when they do find a good one, to treat them right, send them flowers and chocolates. I want them to know that there is a public out there thirsting—dying—for human contact, for a real, honest opinion. And that somebody else besides them "gets it" and cares. Somebody else gives a shit. This is what teaching is. We share our commitment and our excitement. This breeds more excitement. Thus, we pass the torch.

"Our deepest fear is not that we are inadequate. Our deepest fear is that we are powerful beyond measure. It is our light, not our darkness, that most frightens us. We ask ourselves, who am I to be brilliant, gorgeous, talented, and fabulous? Actually, who are you not to be? You are a child of God. Your playing small doesn't serve the world. There's nothing enlightened about shrinking so that other people won't feel insecure around you. We are born to make manifest the glory of God that is within us. It's not just in some of us, it's in everyone. And as we let our own light shine, we unconsciously give other people permission to do the same. As we are liberated

"...from our own fear, our presence automatically liberates others."

—Marianne Williamson, *Return to Love*

41. Watch

Being a designer means, to me at least, having a vision—a way of seeing, an opinion—and applying it to various surfaces and situations. When the Japanese watch company Nuts asked me to design a watch for their designer series, I was at a complete loss. The watch has been a designers' playground for years. There are so many good designs—and too many bad ones. How could I make a watch that was completely mine and have it work as a watch and not just be the expected James Victore cliché?

Working with Nuts offered the perfect opportunity to mix business and pleasure. At 7:20 we feel demure; at 9:10, less so.

42. Time Magazine

It was a privilege to design a cover for *Time*, a magazine that was always in my parents' home and is in mine now. This issue featured five covers by five different designers. Bully for *Time* for reproducing covers that were distinctly not "Time" covers.

As a young designer, I had definite ideas as to who I wished to be down the road. I always thought my ultimate career was to be a cover designer for a major magazine, like Norman Rockwell did for the *Saturday Evening Post*, or my hero George Lois did for *Esquire*. I wanted to be an "agent of change," creating covers to inspire and excite people. But, alas and alack, times, I am told, have changed. Most magazines are fickle and don't commit to long-term relationships with designers. The dictates of contemporary magazine-cover design involve putting the table of contents, a laundry list of everything that might be found inside, on the front, all surrounding a photograph. This tactic was championed years ago by *Reader's Digest*, who found it very successful (read: lucrative), and it has now become the norm. It is a sad state of affairs when a magazine like *Reader's Digest* leads the way.

TIME

The TIME

100

the MOST Influential People in the World

Design for TIME by James Victore

43. Chris Ringland 2002 Shiraz

The wine industry is steeped in tradition. Not until some spunky Californians broke the barrier in 1976 did the world realize there were great and affordable wines from California, Chile, Spain, South Africa, and Australia. Dan Philips, director of the Grateful Palate, is a maverick oenophile who continues to buck tradition in the wine industry, where ugly, fake-vintage wine labels are the norm. Dan and winemaker Chris Ringland not only make a superior product, but they believe in design and its ability to enhance the flavor and experience of their wines.

Ringland owns a small plot of land in Australia's Barossa Valley—forty acres earmarked by God for producing wine. Each year Chris produces four hundred bottles of Shiraz that rank among the best in the world. I was asked to create the announcement that the 2002 Shiraz was available, and was sent one of these ($350) bottles to taste. We opened it and took a sip; it was a cheeky little number. We then let it sit for an hour, and it had magically transformed, had become full and lusty. There were so many discernible flavors:

truffle
licorice
blueberry/blackberry
fresh asphalt
mineral
scorched earth

What I initially wanted to express about the wine was magic, art, and sex. The image, a found object—from a 1950s cheesecake magazine—of a woman kneeling in the dirt, was originally chosen as my own private joke. After tasting the wine, the choice made complete sense. Of course, I knew it all along.

43.1

2002 SHIRAZ "Chris Ringland"
Barossa Valley Score 100

The ugly, hurtful truth.

44. Thoughts on Democracy

In 1943, after Franklin Delano Roosevelt's famous "four freedoms" speech, Norman Rockwell painted his now famous interpretation of said freedoms. *The Saturday Evening Post* reproduced the illustrations on its covers, and the U.S. government even printed and sold sets of the posters to raise $133 million for the war effort. Sadly, time has denigrated the images, rendering them clichés—especially *Freedom from Want* (the family gathered around the table at Thanksgiving).

In 2008, the Wolfsonian Museum at Florida International University invited sixty artists and designers to revisit Rockwell's ideas and create images on the theme of "thoughts on democracy." I have always loved Norman Rockwell's work. His body of work created a portrait of what we could be at our most democratic and American. Asked to create a poster for the show, I chose his *Freedom from Fear*. My response to the assignment came from the idea that the only fear I feel comes from my own country, a place where protest has been deemed unpatriotic. I am fiercely proud of my country, but lack the blind faith necessary to just follow the program. I turned Rockwell's image of proud and caring parents putting their small children to bed (Figure 44.1) into an image of wailing parents pulling an American flag over their son's coffin.

Besides the Wolfsonian Museum's galleries, Thoughts on Democracy was exhibited in two other venues, the Miami International Airport and Miami's Aventura Mall. My poster failed to pass the censors at the two other exhibition venues. I have more than once been censored for my imagery and ideas—reprimanded for either a lack of good taste or amateurism. "Sophomoric" has become my favorite snark. But, meanwhile, nobody complains at the tedium, the boring mediocrity of design and advertising that passes as substance. The pabulum that we accept, flowing down from reputable agencies. Even in design magazines, no one complains about how, for example, all stock photo agency ads look alike—or that stock photo and clip art agencies exist at all.

"Criticism comes easier than craftsmanship."
—Zeuxis, 400 B.C.

44.1

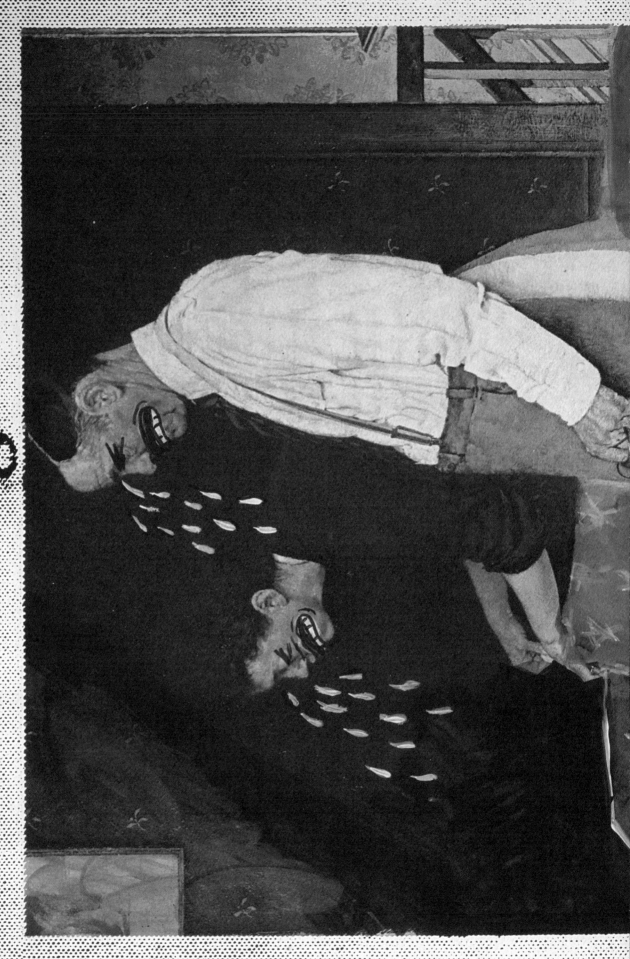

OURS....to fight for

FREEDOM FROM FEAR

Lou: "The main thing about money, Bud, is that it makes you do things you don't want to do." —from *Wall Street*, 1987

45. Sticker Campaign

I love stickers. I have printed thousands of them. I hand them out for free at lectures and workshops. And I find it very telling when a designer or student points out my use of the Cooper Black font or that the apostrophe is actually an inch mark. I don't design these; I order them over the phone. There are only five fonts to choose from, and there is no apostrophe. Questions about the font or grammar or color miss the point completely.

Now, when I say, "Advertisers think you're stupid," I don't mean all advertisers, just most advertisers. And most messages we receive via advertising are a lie. Look at magazine and television advertising. In hopes of creating happy and dedicated consumers, advertisers portray parents as out of touch and stupid, men as incapable morons, and women as castrating shrews. This stereotyping gives us nothing to aspire to; it just creates a rotten model that we congeal to. TV ads, the worst and most prolific culprit, cling to such low standards, coating their messages with either fear or tasteless humor, that we accept this as standard fare. This practiced noncreative behavior is not only tolerated, but it is learned on a mass scale.

Advertisers and designers are social and cultural contributors, if not cultural creators. Thus their work and words and actions have social and cultural meaning. What about consciously creating a culture of excellence? Or just plain talking responsibility for the images and messages we put out?

Remember: Stickering is illegal. Please do it responsibly.

46. Hillman Curtis Box Set

I was once told that a designer is only as good as his or her reference material—as his collection of antique-type books, or her 1950s kitsch clip art. I am only as good as my clients.

Hillman Curtis is a passionate designer, author, musician, and filmmaker, made famous by his books on Web and motion graphics. He is exactly the kind of creator that I am attracted to—he doesn't wait for an invitation; he just makes the work. I first met Hillman when he came to my Brooklyn studio to film me for his series of short documentaries on artists and designers, created for Adobe. By all accounts it is a great little film, but for reasons not apparent to me (these types of reasons are seldom apparent to me, maybe it was the work, maybe the swearing, maybe both), Adobe chose not to support his film of me or run it on their home site.

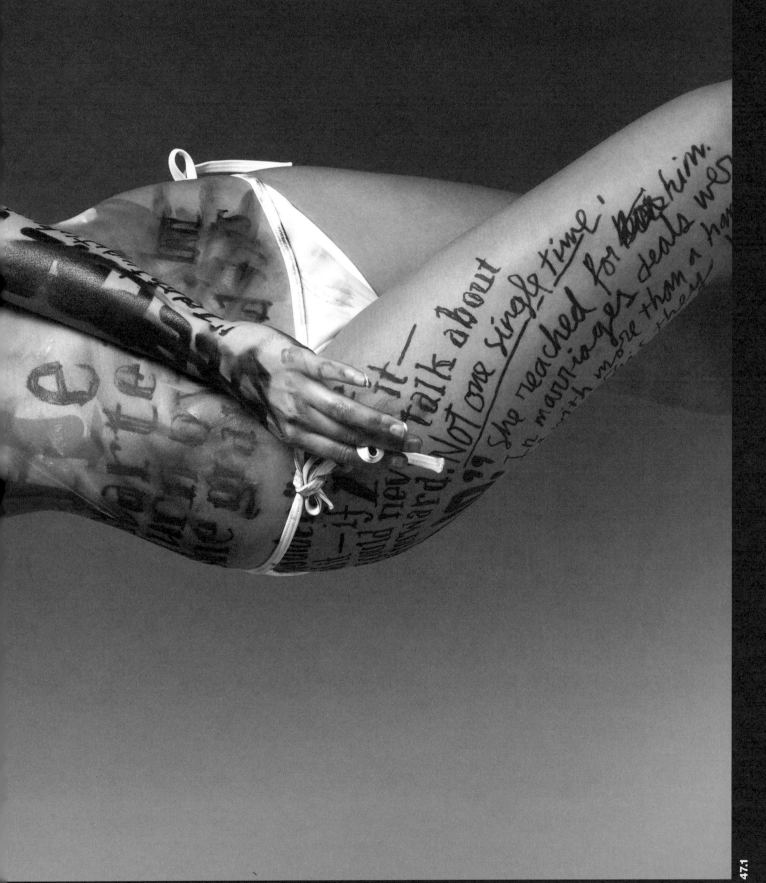

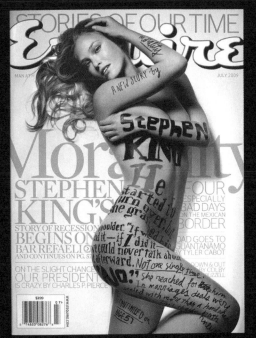

47.2

47. Esquire

You can do hundreds of sketches, but it'll never prepare you for painting on a supermodel. There's no rehearsing, nothing faked, and you only get one shot (except for the unfortunate subsequent Photoshop tweaking). That being said, I did practice. I did hundreds of sketches; I rehearsed on four different models, including a lingerie model and my very patient wife. I also spent hundreds of dollars on makeup and body paint, and became an expert on the subject. But even this did not make the act any less nerve-racking or my hand any less jittery. The model, Bar Refaeli, was a consummate pro. She ignored me completely.

I have the greatest job in the world. Sometimes.

48. How to

I have an unending desire to make images for others.

Invited by the New York AIGA to speak, I chose to talk about this notion in "How to Stay Hard"—a lecture about what it takes to keep me strong and excited. I spoke about personal work, nonclient projects, product design. And love letters. These personal works, made out of devotion, are the most moving, inspired work we as humans make. The best example is from post–9/11 New York, when the streets were full of mementos and tributes honoring the dead or searching for missing loved ones. These came from the heart, not from a formal discipline. No designer could make a response as touching as those made out of need and love. Photoshop is useless here; Illustrator is just a crutch.

The theme of the lecture was the daily effort I make to have creativity in my life. How I use design to tell someone I am thinking of them. I practice constantly; I share design with everyone. I want more designers to love what they do, to understand the importance of and the ability we have to be a positive influence on the world around us—to generate positive, creative change.

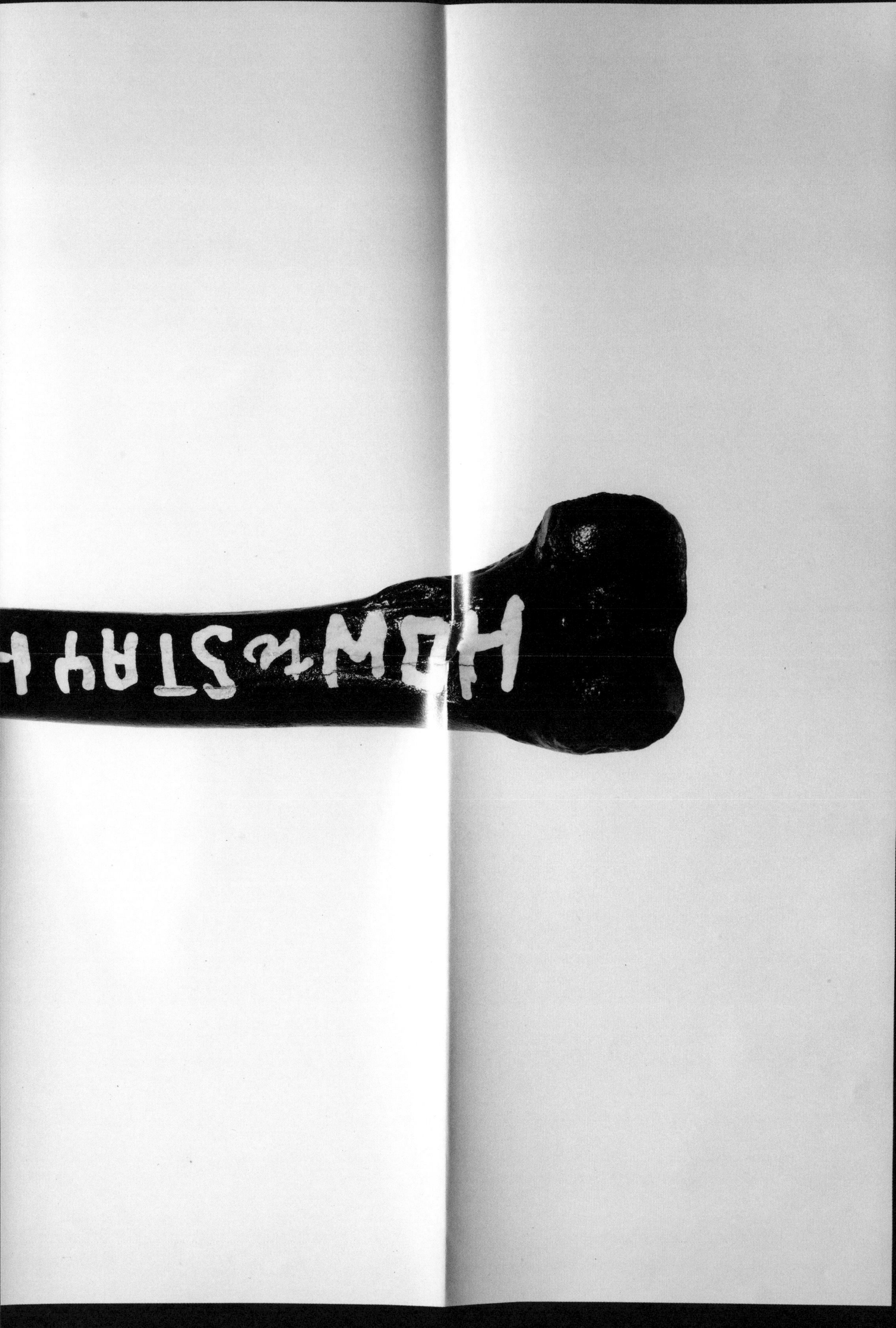
HOW to STAY

Credits

Key:
AD: Art Director
CD: Creative Director

1. Early Book Covers

1.1 *The Amateur Astronomer's Handbook*
Harper and Row
AD: Joseph Montebello
1987

1.2 *Children of Alcoholism*
Harper and Row
AD: Joseph Montebello
1987

1.3 *By Order of the President*
St. Martin's Press
AD: Andy Carpenter
1987

1.4 *The Signet Handbook of Parapsychology*
Signet
1988

1.5 *Largo Desolato*
Harper and Row
AD: Joseph Montebello
1987

1.6 *Master Plan*
Doubleday
1990

1.7 *The Case for Reincarnation*
Carol Publishing/Citadel Press
AD: Steven Brower
1991

1.8 *Kvetch & Acapulco*
Grove Press
1987

1.9 *Ardent Spirits*
Da Capo Press
1992

1.10 *Jazz Spoken Here*
Da Capo Press
1993

1.11 *The Creative Mind*
Carol Publishing/Citadel Press
AD: Steven Brower
1993

1.12 *Encyclopedia of Signs, Omens, and Superstitions*
Carol Publishing/Citadel Press
AD: Steven Brower
1992

1.13 *The Talisman Magick Workbook*
Carol Publishing/Citadel Press
AD: Steven Brower
1992

1.14 *Tales of Beatnik Glory*
Carol Publishing/Citadel Press
AD: Steven Brower
1989

1.15 *Johnny Got His Gun*
Carol Publishing/Citadel Press
AD: Steven Brower
1991

1.16 *Advanced Backstabbing and Mudslinging Techniques*
Carol Publishing/Citadel Press
AD: Steven Brower
1991

1.17 *The Werewolf of Paris*
Carol Publishing/Citadel Press
AD: Steven Brower
1991

1.18 *Mayhem*
Carol Publishing/Citadel Press
AD: Steven Brower
1992

1.19 *The Secrets of Love Magick*
Carol Publishing/Citadel Press
AD: Steven Brower
1992

1.20 *The Crazy Green of Second Avenue*
Carol Publishing/Citadel Press
AD: Steven Brower
1993

1.21 *Revenge Tactics from the Master*
Carol Publishing/Citadel Press
AD: Steven Brower
1994

1.22 *Hélène Cixous*
Columbia University Press
AD: Teresa Bonner
1994

1.23 *Guernica and Other Plays*
Grove Press
AD: John Gall
1995

1.24 *What Is Philosophy?*
Columbia University Press
AD: Teresa Bonner
1994

1.25 *Mea Cuba*
Farrar, Straus and Giroux
AD: Michael Ian Kaye
1995

2. Early Promotional Cards
Self-authored
6 x 4"
1985–95

3. Greeting Cards
Rohnart
AD: Joseph DiSimone
Foil Stamp
1989–93

4. Celebrate Columbus

4.1 Celebrate Columbus
Printer Mechanical

4.2 Celebrate Columbus
Cultural poster
Self-authored
Photo: Alexander Gardner, 1872
Offset
35.5 x 23.75"
1992

5. Racism
Social poster
Self-authored
Silkscreen
26 x 40"
1993

6. Double Justice
Film poster

6.1 Front
6.2 Back
NAACP/LDF and ACLU
AD: Kica Matos
Offset
32.5 x 23"
1993

7. The Shakespeare Project
Theater posters
CD: Scott Cargle
1993–2000

7.1 Venus & Adonis
Silkscreen
38 x 25"
2000

7.2 Twelfth Night
Silkscreen
40.5 x 26.5"
1994

7.3 Romeo and Juliet

7.4 Outdoor
Offset/Silkscreen
38 x 25"
1993

7.5 Coriolanus (outdoor)
Silkscreen
38 x 25"
1996

7.6 Macbeth
Silkscreen
33.75 x 23.75"
1995

22.1 Images, Politics and Cross-pollination
Lecture poster
Client: Syracuse University
Silkscreen
25 x 38"
1997

22.2 Disney Go Home
Silkscreen
38 x 25"
1999

22.3 Just Say No
Silkscreen
38 x 25"
1999

23. Choose or Lose
Political poster

23.1 Al Gore Image Copyright
Diana Walker

23.2 Choose or Lose
MTV
CD: Jeffrey Keyton
Offset
36 x 26"
2000

24. Moët & Chandon
Advertising poster
Moët & Chandon
CD: Alain Weill
Offset
39.5 x 27.5"
2000

25. Come

25.1 Come
Invitation/postcard
AIGA
CD: Adams Morioka
6 x 9"
2001

25.2 9/11 Photo Copyright of
Robert Clark

26. Mad as Hell

26.1 Lecture poster
AIGANY
CD: Carin Goldberg
Photo: Tom Schierlitz
Offset
39 x 26"
2002

26.2 Video Stills Copyright Gary Leib

27. Nouveau Salon des Cent
Exhibition poster
CD: Anthon Beeke
Photo: Tom Schierlitz
Offset
38.5 x 26.75"
2001

28. Bush Pirate
Political poster
AIGANY/International A.N.S.W.E.R.
Silkscreen
32 x 46"
2003

29. SVA
Subway posters/advertising
Visual Arts Press
CD: Silas Rhodes

29.1 Art Is . . .
Offset
46 x 30"
1996

29.2 Beach Family
Graffiti: Matthew McGuinness
Offset
46 x 30"
2002

29.3 Magic
Photo: Tom Schierlitz
Offset
46 x 30"
2004

29.4 Rilke
Offset
46 x 30"
2007

30. Urgent Action

30.1 Identity package
Amnesty International
CD: Helen Garrett
2000

30.2 Urgent Action poster/direct mail
Offset
22 x 17"
2000

31. Medea
Broadway poster/campaign
SpotCo
CD: Drew Hodges
Various sizes
2002

32. Aveda

32.1 Campaign for "Earth Month"
Aveda
AD: Enoch Palmer
Offset
Various sizes
2005

32.2 In store

33. Hero/Victim
Exhibition, gallery buttons
"Armour: The Fortification of Man"
Fort Asperen, the Netherlands
AD: Li Edelkoort
2.25" diameter
2003

34. Chronogram
Magazine cover
Chronogram magazine
AD: Carla Rozman
2005

35. Aristocrats (Killed)
Magazine page
GQ magazine
Photo: Tom Schierlitz
2005

36. Plates
Self-authored

36.1 Poster
Silkscreen
36 x 24"

36.2 Milton
10" diameter

36.3 Various sizes

37. Blackpool
Magazine cover
Blackpool magazine
AD: Benjamin Raimbault
2009

38. Yohji
Marketing/promotional materials
Yohji Yamamoto Homme
CD: Yohji Yamamoto
AD: Coralie Gautier
2007–09

38.1 Postcards
Silkscreen
6 x 9"

38.2 Poster
Chapeau
Offset
16 x 22"

38.3 Poster
Spring/Summer '09
Offset
22 x 16"

39. Surf
Hand-painted surfboards

39.1 Smoker
Shaper: Mike Becker, Natures Shapes
Photo: Tom Schierlitz
9' 6"
2007

39.2 Peligrosas Que Curvas
Y Yo Sin Frenos!
Hand-painted original

Acknowledgments

To my editor deluxe, Deborah Aaronson, thank you for both your camaraderie and your ruthless honesty. To all my friends at Harry N. Abrams, thank you for taking a chance on me and this book. To Paul Sahre—a good father and a good friend—for his vision, hard work, counsel, and design, I am eternally indebted. To Michael Bierut for his neatly typed introduction. A great thank you to Robert Hunt for contributing his artistry to my cover. To Tom Schierlitz for his consistent support and friendship—your photographs make my work look better. To Bruce and Violaine Bernard, merci de votre assistance et votre amitié.

To all those who have made an impact in my life (somewhat chronologically): To my parents, Joseph and Rosalie Victore—your influence and humor is what made this work possible. To my sisters, Anne Marie McManus and Jacqueline Stein, my biggest fans and collectors. And to Laurie Dolphin, my other sister. To Leah Lococo, thank you for your friendship and understanding and for our beautiful boy, Luca. And to Luca Victore, my most important work and best friend, to whom this book is dedicated.

A belated thank you to Pat Duniho, who introduced me to graphic design, and to Gary Danko, the first truly creative person I ever met, who pointed me in the direction of New York City. To Henryk Tomaszewski, whose work first illuminated the world of graphic design to me, and to Pierre Bernard, my mentor and friend, who showed me what was possible with ink on paper, I will always be grateful. To Paul Bacon, my other father. To Joseph Montebello, who took a chance on me and gave me my first job, and to Steven Brower, who showed me how we are supposed to do it. To Steven Heller, thank you for your example of excellence. To Richard Wilde, my chairman at the School of Visual Arts, whose strength amazes me and whose guidance brightens the path. To SVA and the Rhodes family, thank you for your patronage and the creative opportunities you've given me. To Gemma Gatti, our long-standing relationship has helped me grow personally and professionally; and to Hank Richardson for his insight and relentless conviction to his students. To Ray Brunner for his faith and trust in my work, and to all the Design Within Reach folks, who encourage me to keep moving forward.

I am forever thankful to my droogs, whom I count on unflinchingly: Nicholas Blechman, Marc Burckhardt, Alan Dye, John Fulbrook, Christian Helms, Ross MacDonald, Matt McGuinness, Christoph Niemann, Brian Rea, Stefan Sagmeister, Morgan Sheasby, Dan VanHoozer, the aforementioned Paul Sahre, and Tom Schierlitz.

A kind thank you to all those who helped shape this book through its words, pictures, or shape: Chris Thompson, Grant Gold, Mika Osborne, Joanna Ahlberg, Fanny LeBras, Sebastian Rether, Leah Horowitz, Rachel Matts, Lauren Schoonover, Jonas Beuchert, Najung Kim, and David Womack.

The work herein comes from my studio, a combination of myself and a revolving team of creative hotheads too numerous to mention here. To all the past members of the team, I owe a debt of gratitude. You are all kings and queens.

Thanks to the parks and bars around Brooklyn that gave me the elbow room to write this book, and the folks there, especially Sam and the gang at Nita Nita. And finally to my wife, Laura Victore, thank you for your excitement, your tolerance, your patience, your rainbows, and your sunshine. As for the facts and dates and historical accuracy of the stories I've included, I did my best to ensure their veracity. My apologies to any who remember them differently. Fudge happens.

39.3 Peligrosas Que Curvas
Y Yo Sin Frenos!
Design Within Reach
Shaper: Mike Becker, Natures Shapes
CD: Ray Brunner
Limited Edition, 6' 2"
DWR photo Copyright Mark Seelen
2008

40. Teaching
SVA photo Copyright David Corio

41. Watch
Watch design
Nuts, Japan
CD: Bruce Osborne
Photo: Yasuhide Numao
2009

42. Time
Magazine cover
Time magazine
AD: Arthur Hochstein
2008

43. Chris Ringland
Advertising poster/direct-mail kit
Chris Ringland, R Wines
CD: Dan Phillips
AD: Beth Elliot

43.1 Direct-mail kit

43.2 Poster
Offset
48 x 34"
2008

44. Thoughts on Democracy
Political poster
The Wolfsonian Museum
CD: Cathy Leff
AD: Tim Hossler

44.1 Freedom from Fear Printed by permission of the Norman Rockwell Family Agency
Copyright © 1943 The Norman Rockwell Family Entities

44.2 Digital print
20 x 15.25" and 48 x 34"
2008

45. Advertisers Think You're Stupid
Stickers
Self-authored
5 x 3"
2005–
George Washington courtesy of O.O.P.S

46. Hillman Curtis Box Set
DVD packaging
Hillman Curtis, Inc.
CD: Hillman Curtis
Illustrator: Wil Freeborn
Letterpress
2009

47. Esquire
Magazine cover/interior
Esquire magazine
CD: David Curcurito
Photo Ed: Michael Norseng
Photo: James White
Model: Bar Refaeli
2009

47.1 Interior

47.2 Esquire cover

48. How To
Lecture poster
AIGANY
CD: Drew Hodges
Photo: Tom Schierlitz
Offset
22.5 x 34"
2009

* MoMA letter
Please note: This is not the "official" letter of acceptance from the museum.

The Museum of Modern Art   **Department of Architecture and Design**

November 11, 2008

James Victore's Mom
36 South 4th Street
Studio D3
Brooklyn, NY 11211

Dear James Victore's Mom,

It is with great pleasure that I write to inform you that on November 10, 2008 the Architecture &
Design Acquisition Committee decided to add nine of your son's posters to the permanent
collection of the Museum of Modern Art.   In addition, several of James' posters will be exhibited in
the upcoming exhibition *Rough Cut: Design Takes a Sharp Edge,* opening November 26, 2008.
I invite you to stop by and see your boy's work, and other works from our collection on display in
the museum galleries – just let us know and we will arrange some complimentary tickets for you.

I hope you will join me in congratulating your son on this great news.

Best regards,

Paul Galloway
Cataloguer